Living Feng Shui
Personal Stories

Living Feng Shui
Personal Stories

Carole J. Hyder

Hyder Enterprises, Inc.
Minneapolis

Revised and redesigned new first edition.

To order this book, or *Wind and Water: Your Personal Feng Shui Journey,* or DVDs, go to Carole's website www.carolehyder.com

.

Published by Hyder Enterprises, Inc.

Book design: Dorie McClelland, Spring Book Design

Back cover photo: Ann Marsden

Publisher's Cataloging-in-Publication available on request

ISBN 978-0-966-4434-3-1

Printed and bound in India by Replika Press Pvt. Ltd.

To all the people
who have so generously taught me
and continue to teach me about
living Feng Shui

Contents

Stories

Welcome to a new edition

With pride I present my second book in its originally intended design, subscribing to the look and feel my designer and I had carefully constructed to conform to good Feng Shui principles. I hope you'll enjoy its new package.

In 1998, I wrote my first book *Wind and Water: Your Personal Feng Shui Journey*. The response was overwhelming. I heard from people all over the world about how the book impacted them. Its format was simple. A reader could integrate the book page by page, or issue by issue. Or they could begin on page one and read straight through to the end. However they did it, people were touched.

I continued my Feng Shui work with clients and had the privilege of being involved very intimately with many open and heart-centered individuals. As a result I was inspired to write again. This time my intention was to provide real-life case studies of how people were living in their spaces. The principles from the first book are now applied in practical ways in this second publication *Living Feng Shui: Personal Stories*.

The names have been changed in each of the stories. But the situations and results are true. Where relevant to the story, I have included my working drawings. These are not intended to be architectural renderings or blueprints, but simply illustrations to enhance the reader's understanding.

Living Feng Shui

This book, along with my first one, would never have seen the light of day had it not been for Professor Thomas Lin Yun. A Buddhist teacher, he beautifully blends our Western mind-set with the traditional principles of Feng Shui. Only through his efforts, his insights, and his wisdom are we able to take advantage of this information and put it to work. I invite you to ponder the calligraphy blessings he sent me that appear at the front of this book.

My subsequent studies with master teacher Roger Green have succeeded in deepening my understanding of the power and subtleties of Feng Shui.

I owe a huge thank you to my designer Dorie McClelland who infused the book with her magic—again. She so remarkably orchestrates the energy around these stories that we end up with a final product of exquisite design and beauty. But then, I expect nothing less from her.

My husband Tom unselfishly lent his time and energy to this project. Uncomplainingly he read and re-read the stories, lovingly offering his opinions and suggestions. A lifetime of gratitude is due him for being my support, my friend, and for living Feng Shui with me.

I am blessed to have Feng Shui in my life, not only for what it has done for me but for the countless opportunities to work so personally and deeply with others, to witness the changes they bravely put into place, and to celebrate with them in the end. Herein are a few of these poignant personal journeys.

Foreword

Professor Thomas Lin Yun

The Chinese have an ancient proverb: "It is better to be happy (or to share the happiness) with a crowd than to be happy alone." After I read Carole Hyder's new book, I made some reflections. Even though she is already a scholarly expert, when she was attending my workshops she was totally devoted to her study of Feng Shui so that "the indigo ink is bluer than the indigo plant from which it comes."* To put it simply, when Carole studied Feng Shui, she did it wholeheartedly and with diligence. After she acquired the necessary skills, she was then able to help those people in society who need Feng Shui adjustment. Finally, she carefully made records of case studies and made an accurate and honest account of the truth before and after Black Sect Tantric Buddhist Feng Shui adjustment.

Therefore, Carole would have an in-depth understanding of the power of Black Sect Tantric Buddhist Feng Shui perspective. Her abilities and her success allowed her to have an indescribable happiness and comfort that stemmed from deep in her heart. Carole has turned this emotional happiness into words and wrote this new book. Once published, this will allow her clients, beneficiaries, relatives and friends, and those readers who don't understand Feng Shui to acquire an immediate resonance. This is why I said that Carole exalted the spirit and love of "it is better to be happy with a crowd than to be happy alone." She had written this great book that is very clear and easy to understand.

There are many positive aspects to this book. For example, every chapter uses actual case studies as its content. Every case study is made clearer with illustrations of the floor plan. The comparative studies before and after Feng Shui adjustments are also another specialty of this book. However, in order to protect the privacy of the actual clients, their names and identities had to be changed. If it was possible to reveal the actual year, month, date and hour, and the actual area where these houses, apartments and office buildings were located, then it would enable the reader to understand even more clearly that this is absolute truth being chronicled. Even though this book does not introduce Feng Shui through theory, logic, or historical lineage, these actual Feng Shui case studies allow the reader to cross all barriers and immediately immerse in the phenomenon of Feng Shui. This kind of experience is much more advanced and direct than traditional teaching methods used in classrooms.

The narration of a good book does not rely on clear penmanship or rich content. There should also be good writing techniques, careful arrangement, love and inspiration in order to present a good and solid publication. Some books have good wording, but the content is too profound to be understood. Some books have smooth penmanship, but the content is rather empty. Some books have good wording and good content, but the effect of the writing skills is lost due to not understanding the readers' needs. Carole's new book is carefully designed so that is has all of the above stated advantages and none of the above stated shortcomings. This is another special value that sets it apart from other publications. I have strong faith that the readers will share my same sentiment.

*This is a proverb that means that the student is so diligent that his achievements surpass that of his teacher. This is a humble expression often used by teachers to show their humility.

Translated from Chinese by Mary R. Hsu

Calligraphy

The greatest gift a student can receive from their teacher is their blessing for the work that they're doing following in the footsteps of the teacher. As a student of Professor Thomas Lin Yun, I requested his blessing of this book of stories. In typical fashion, he generously forwarded to me the following calligraphy pieces, done by his own hand. It is with great honor that I share these with the reader so everyone can benefit from his benedictions.

Professor Thomas Lin Yun created six pieces of calligraphy after reading the manuscript for this book. Following are the texts that came with each, referred to by their number. The words are Professor Lin Yun's, translated from Chinese by Mary R. Hsu.

Figure I
(from right to left)

Right: Written while chanting infinite numbers of mantras on the day of the Mid-Autumn Festival, Year 2000, to bestow blessing upon benevolent persons with good karma and the readers of Carole Hyder's new masterpiece which benefits the world.

Center: Calligraphy, "Opening this book will bring great benefits."

Left: Composed by the Master of *Yun Shi Jing She*,* Lin Yun, while a visitor at the study of disciple Crystal Chu in Berkeley, California.

*Note: *Yun Shi Jing She* is the name of Grandmaster Professor Lin Yun's shrines and sanctuaries all over the world.

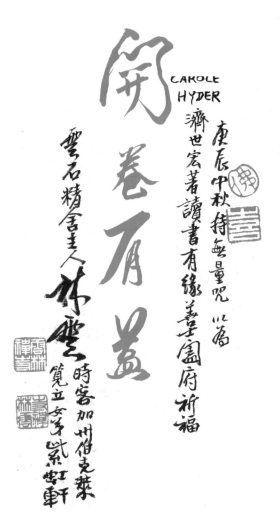

CAROLE
HYDER

Figure 1

Calligraphy by Professor Thomas Lin Yun

Figure 2

(from top to bottom)

Top: Calligraphy of the Chinese character "Tao." In smaller script is the definition of Tao according to Black Sect Tantric Buddhism: A Yin and a Yang combine as one, thereby following the laws of nature and set in motion continuously. Also in small script is the "Six-Syllable Mantra: Om Ma Ni Pad Me Hum." Written by Lin Yun while chanting mantras.

Center: Symbol of the *Yin-Yang*, with smaller symbols of the *Yin-Yang* contained within. According to Grandmaster Professor Lin Yun, there is *Yin* in *Yang*, and there is *Yang* in *Yin*. Within the *Yang* that is in *Yin*, there is another set of *Yin-Yang*, and the same within the *Yin* that is in *Yang*, and so on.

Bottom right: There is *Yang* in *Yin*, and there is *Yin* in *Yang*. When *Yin* and *Yang* are in harmony, then there will be world peace. Composed by the Master of *"Yun Shr Hsuan,"* Lin Yun, while a visitor at the study of disciple Chun-Hui Yu.

Bottom left: Written while chanting infinite numbers of mantras on the day of the Mid-Autumn Festival in the Year 2000. To bestow blessing and wisdom upon the readers, author, and publisher of Carole Hyder's new masterpiece.

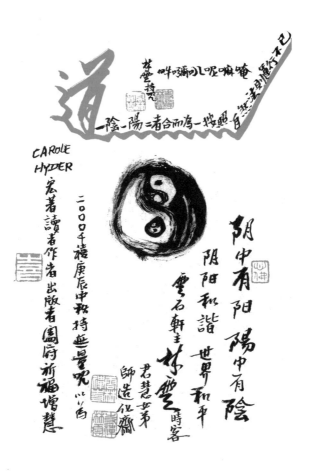

Figure 2

Calligraphy by Professor Thomas Lin Yun

Figure 3

(from right to left)

Right: Written on the day of the Mid-Autumn Festival in the Year 2000 after offering incense and chanting mantras, to bestow blessing upon the readers, author, and publisher of Carole Hyder's new masterpiece. May they and their family members receive happiness, wealth, good health, and peace.

Center: Talisman

(from top to bottom)

"The Divine order by the highest Taoist deity to immediately offer protection."

"The Five Thunder Protectors Mantra"

"The Eight Trigrams, or the *Bagua*"

"The Six-Syllable Mantra: Omm Ma Ni Pad Me Hum"

"Tracing of the Nine Star Path"

In the right circles: This Talisman will offer protection to the home of a person with auspicious karma.

In the left circles: Wealth will arrive at the home of a benevolent and kind person.

Left: Composed by the Master of *Yun Shi Jin She,** Lin Yun, while a visitor at the study of disciple Crystal Chu.

*Note: *Yun Shi Jing She* is the name of Grandmaster Professor Lin Yun's shrines and sanctuaries all over the world.

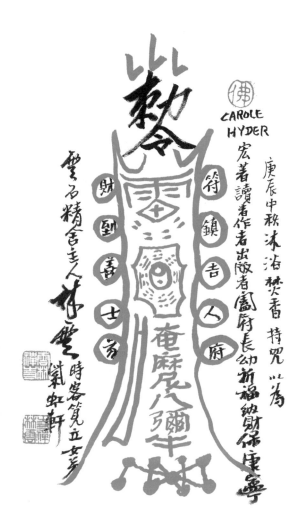

Figure 3

Calligraphy by Professor Thomas Lin Yun

Figure 4

(from top to bottom)

Top: A Hidden Title Poem. In Chinese, the first characters of each line, read horizontally from right to left, says, "Feng Shui and Nature, when Harmonious, is the Best."

> Tigers appear in wind
> Dragons emerge from clouds
> These images seem real yet untrue
> Water is clear, and trees are lush
> From this we can sense vital energy
> Freedom and ease fill the heaven and earth
> Whether this is true or not
> After we have analyzed it, we will obtain new knowledge
> Peace and warfare are spread equally throughout the world
> Just as humor and seriousness also fill the entire universe
> The ultimate is when karma begins and karma ceases
> So it is best to spread this teaching to all who would like to know.

Bottom right: Written on the day of the Mid-Autumn Festival in the Year 2000 to be presented to the readers, author, and publisher of Carole Hyder's new masterpiece.

Bottom center: Calligraphy, "Feng Shui."

Bottom left: Composed by Lin Yun, the "Recluse Scholar Who Emerges with the Dragon," wile a visitor at the study of disciple Belle Tao.

風虎雲龍假亦真
水清樹茂見精神
自由自在充天地
然否否然格物新
和戰平分全世界
諧莊佈滿大乾坤
最是緣生緣滅處
好將大道告知音

風水

CAROLE HYDER

宏著讀者作者出版者

庚辰中秋 詩贈

從龍山人 林雲 時客方圓 女弟樂陶居

Figure 4

Calligraphy by Professor Thomas Lin Yun

*Note: In the Chinese tradition, it is very common for scholars to have many names or aliases. In ancient Chinese folklore, tigers and dragons are regarded as mystical creatures so that when they appear, it was always with some form of natural phenomenon such as whirling winds or puffs of clouds, respectively. Since the word "Yun" in Grandmaster Professor Lin Yun's name means "cloud," he has chosen the "Recluse Scholar that Emerges with the Dragon (Tsong Long Shan Ren)" as one of his numerous scholarly names.

Figure 5

(from right to left)

Right: Written with cinnabar while adding the Three Secret Reinforcements, on the day of the Mid-Autumn Festival in the Year 2000. An old poetic work is written here to be shared with the readers of Carole Hyder's new masterpiece which brings great benefits to the world.

Top center: Calligraphy, "Three Secret Reinforcements."

Bottom center: Poem

If you want your secret cures to be effective

First of all you have got to have faith

If your visualization lacks respect and piety

You'll come up empty even with the Three Secret Reinforcements.

Left: Composed by Lin Yun of Black Sect Tantric Buddhism's First Temple, the Yun Lin Temple, while a visitor at the study of disciple Lynn Ho To.

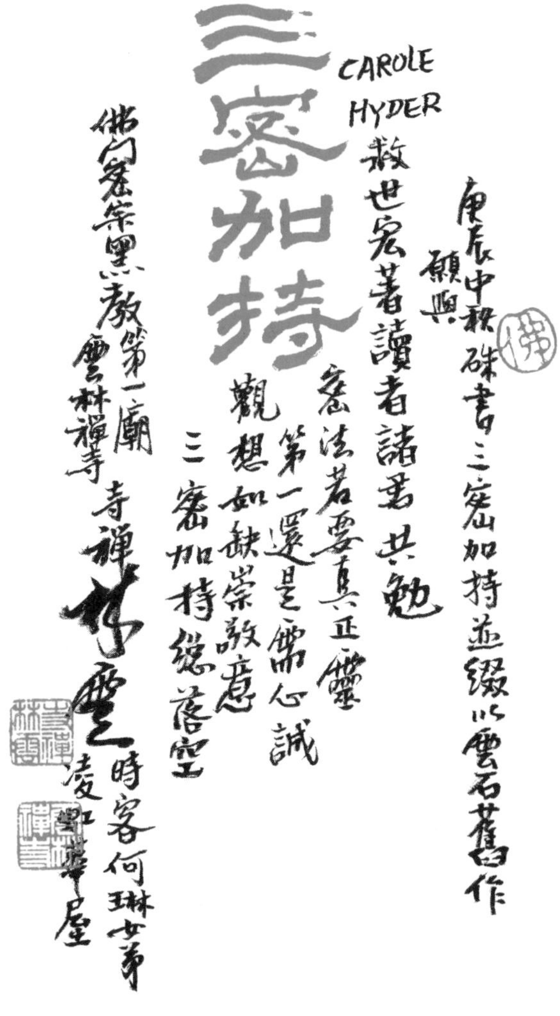

Figure 5

Calligraphy by Professor Thomas Lin Yun

Figure 6

(from right to left)

Right: Written with cinnabar while chanting the highest order mantras, on the day of the Mid-Autumn Festival in the Year of the Golden Dragon, 2000. An old poetic work is written here to be shared with the readers of Carole Hyder's new masterpiece which brings great benefits to the world.

Top center: Calligraphy, "Enlightenment."

Bottom center: Poem

> Who is the winner, and who shall lose?
>
> Even the smart one is eventually confused.
>
> My advice to you is to read between the lines,
>
> And ponder the wonders of the hidden meanings.

Left: Composed by Lin Yun of Black Sect Tantric Buddhism's Second Temple, the Lin Yun Monastery, while a visitor at the study of disciple Robert Chiu.

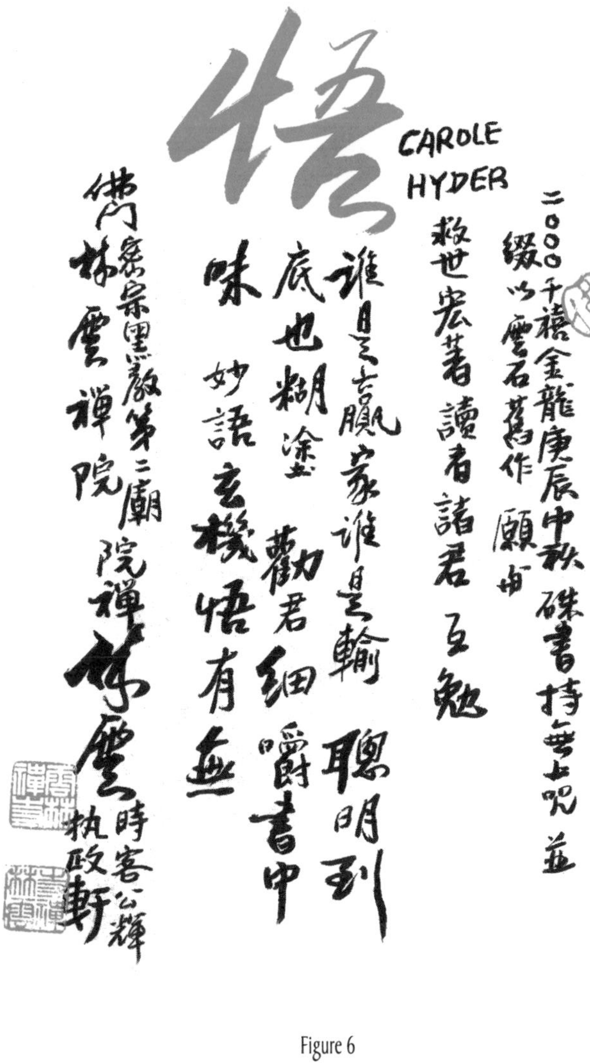

悟

CAROLE HYDER

佛門密宗墨教第三屆

林雲禪院

院禪林雲

執政軒

時客公輝

禪林雲書

禪林雲書

誰是玄贏　家誰是輸　聰明到

底也糊塗　勸君細嚼書中

味　妙語玄機悟有無

二〇〇〇千禧金龍庚辰中秋　碟書持無上咒並

綴以雲石爲作　願由

救世宏著讀者諸君互勉

Figure 6

Calligraphy by Professor Thomas Lin Yun

Feng Shui

Feng Shui

What is Feng Shui?

Feng Shui can give you a new perspective for looking at
the spaces where you work and where you live. Because
one of the basic principles of Feng Shui is that your space mirrors
your life, it would follow that you would get a new perspective on
your life by using Feng Shui tools. Feng Shui can provide ways to
create a space to bring about prosperity, productivity, partners, and
peace. By incorporating some of the simplest and smallest suggestions, it is not hard to realize the power of Feng Shui.

In most cases, the adjustments for Feng Shui are subtle and afford-
able. Sometimes the adjustment is not even visible, such as placing a
small mirror behind a painting or in a closet, or placing coins in the
foundation of a new building. The power of the adjustment does not
depend on the object as much as the intention with which the object
is placed. The stronger the intent, the more dramatic the results.

Analyzing a space

There are three ways in which to analyze a space with regard to
Feng Shui. One way is to assess the shape of the building, the house,
or a room. It is ideal to have a simple and uncomplicated system of
walls that holds your life together. The more structural angles and

complications in a space, the more activity the occupants' lives will take on. Less is more.

Another way is to look at what you own, how much you own, and where you put it. In considering this, it may be necessary for you to deal with some clutter issues. In Feng Shui, everything is energy. The more possessions you have, the more energy is required to maintain them or keep them. Sometimes changing the position of a sofa and chairs can create a more conversational arrangement, opening up lines of communication between family members. Sometimes changing the location of the bed can enable someone to sleep better. Sometimes de-cluttering a countertop or a desk can open up new channels to creativity and clear thinking. Again, less is more.

Finally, you can check out the layout of a space based on a mental map called a *bagua*, to determine the placement of nine life issues. When a bagua is appropriately placed and enhanced, your life begins to manifest good fortune and blessed occurrences. The nine areas of the bagua are shown on the next page.

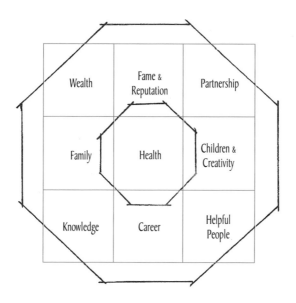

The front door

You can place this mental map over the main floor of a building or a home, an individual room, even a desktop. The orientation of the bagua is determined by the position of the front door. The front door, however, may not be the door you use all of the time. Nevertheless, the entrance that was architecturally intended to be the front door is the one with which you will work. The front entrance is usually in the Knowledge, Career, or Helpful People area.

Knowledge door   Career door   Helpful People door

If you look at your space as though flying above it, include in the bagua anything that has a roof and sides. Therefore, include an attached garage or a screened-in porch in the layout. A deck and overhangs are not part of the bagua because they do not have both a roof and sides.

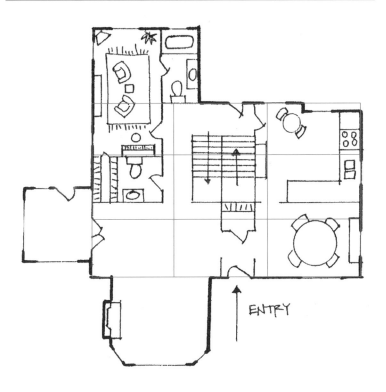

ENTRY

Example 2
The bagua superimposed over a house

Missing pieces and extensions

You will probably realize that your house is not a perfect square or rectangle. In all likelihood, it will have some pieces protruding and some missing. When a piece is missing, it indicates a depletion or challenge in that bagua area. You want to "capture" missing areas by planting a tree in the corner, installing a flagpole or light post, positioning a fountain or birdbath, running a fence around the area, or creating any marker that will reinforce your intention to complete what is missing.

If you have little pieces protruding from the main part of your house, you have an extension in the corresponding area of the bagua.

An extension is auspicious and gives you extra energy in that particular area. Extensions do not need to be changed or adjusted. See the examples on the following page.

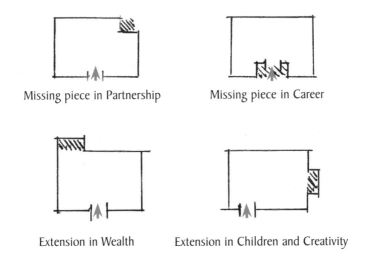

Missing piece in Partnership

Missing piece in Career

Extension in Wealth

Extension in Children and Creativity

Individual rooms

There are times when it is difficult to determine which way the bagua lays out. For example, you may have a door that doesn't face the street or a slanted door. It may be easier to incorporate the Feng Shui bagua on a room-by-room basis. When you lay out a bagua over an individual room, determine the front entry to the room. If you have more than one entrance into a room, the front entry is the one used most frequently or the one closest to the main front door. The bagua areas of an individual room could be in a different orientation than the bagua of the main floor. It is not important that they match. You can also superimpose the bagua over your desk and your bed. See example 3 on the following page.

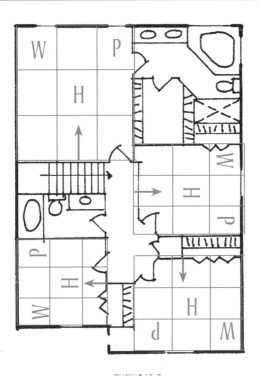

The bagua superimposed over individual rooms in different orientations.
The "H" designates the Health area.
The "W" designates the Wealth area.
The "P" designates the Partnership area.

Color

Each area of the bagua is not only represented by a life issue but also by a color. The color, or its variation, can be used in the corresponding part of the bagua. For example, if Wealth is a problem, you can integrate something purple, lavender, magenta, or mauve in that area. Because colors are so personal, it is very important that you use a color you love, otherwise don't use the color at all.

Explanation of the areas of the bagua

Career

A career represents your abilities, talents, and interests. A career takes you from one phase of your life to the next. It is a vehicle for your passion, even if you don't get paid for it. Many people find enjoyment in their paying professions, yet they also love to volunteer, garden, or paint. All of these are activities and directions for your pursuits and are classified under the Career area of the bagua.

Knowledge

The area of Knowledge is about learning and education in whatever form that may take for you—a high school diploma, a graduate degree, a certification or license in a field of interest, or simply reading up on a topic. It can also be about your children's educational issues. It further

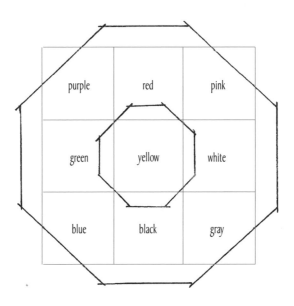

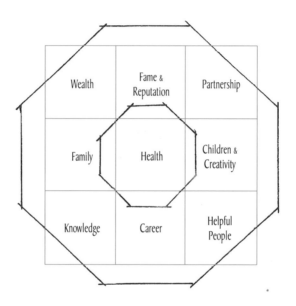

reflects the ascent to higher self-knowledge, learning about yourself. It also reflects the undertaking to share your knowledge or information with others.

Family
Family issues include your family of origin such as parents, siblings, cousins, and relations. It also includes anyone you consider your extended family, such as good friends, neighbors, and colleagues. This area is most commonly recognized as dealing with your roots and where you came from. It also reflects any groups brought together for a specific purpose, such as work teams, church groups, or committees.

Wealth
Wealth is about your money, both coming in and going out. How you get your money (wages, lottery, inheritance, stocks, gifts, funding) balances how you spend your money (expenses, gifts, charity, inheritance, retirement).

Fame and Reputation
The Fame and Reputation area stands for your image and how the world sees you. It represents your good name and your standing in the community. In a business setting, it reflects your connection to the outside world and community, and becoming known for what you do.

Partnership

The Partnership area represents personal partners, business partners, spiritual partners, and partnering with yourself. Getting to know yourself or working through some issues with a partner fall into this category.

Children and Creativity

Children and Creativity stands for your own children, other children you may be involved with, and your inner child. It includes anything which you may "birth" in your life in addition to children—a book, a thesis, poetry, music, your stories.

Helpful People

Helpful People are often referred to as angels, particularly when they show up unexpectedly with exactly what you need when you need it. Helpful people are those who support you emotionally and sometimes financially. They can be a best friend, a relative, a minister, a plumber. A helpful person can be a real estate agent who helps you sell your house or a travel agent who gets you from here to there. A helpful person can be a client for your business. As part of the ebb and flow of Feng Shui, being a helpful person is as important as having helpful people or benefactors in your life. Sometimes you need to be one before you will see any benefactors in your own life.

Health

The center of the bagua is the Health area. This area represents health on physical, mental, emotional, and spiritual levels. By placing Health in the center, a hub or core is created around which everything else revolves. It follows that if you are not feeling well, you do not do your job well; you do not relate to your partner or children in a patient, loving manner; your productivity and creativity are affected; your pay may even be affected. Feeling well can support functioning well.

Stories

Ray and Angela

Building a dream

I was called by a couple, Ray and
Angela, who were looking to build a
home. They had their blueprints from the architect and wanted me to
look at them. Unfortunately, they were on their final draft and were
not too open to many changes. Their architect had been invited to
our meeting but declined. His perspective was that Feng Shui would
only complicate their process which had been going smoothly. Additionally, there was no scientific proof, according to him, that adding
any Feng Shui adjustments would make any positive difference. Nevertheless, Ray and Angela wanted another perspective, yet quietly
hoped I wouldn't suggest they change anything.

Building a dream

Ray and Angela were empty nesters. All of their children were grown and married. However, they were moving from a smaller home to this bigger one. Now that their four children were having children of their own, they could provide a gathering place for all of them during the holidays or at other times of the year. Because their children were living in different parts of the world, Ray and Angela wanted to give them a place they and their families could always return for a short or an extended visit. They had built an apartment above their garage for these occasions.

Ray had taken early retirement so Angela and he could travel. Despite good investments and a generous retirement package, they were concerned about having enough money to last them the rest of their years. Although they were both in fairly good health, Ray had been experiencing digestive problems.

When I looked at their layout according to the bagua (see *Proposed Plan*), it was clear to me that Ray and Angela were building a home with their children in mind. The Children and Creativity area was extended out beyond normal boundaries indicating extra energy around this issue. The garage was an over-sized piece added onto the house, coming off the Knowledge area. I asked about their youngest son. Angela looked surprised that I would ask about him as it was this

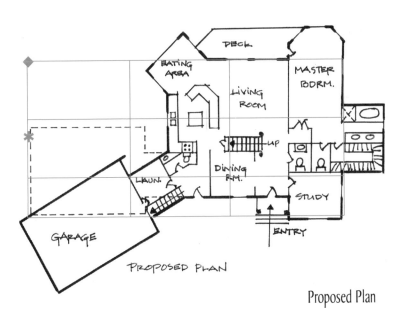

DECK

EATING AREA

LIVING ROOM

MASTER BDRM.

UP

DINING RM.

LAUN.

STUDY

GARAGE

ENTRY

PROPOSED PLAN

Proposed Plan

child who would probably be using the guest area the most. He had three children of his own, lived the farthest away, and was the one most likely to visit on a regular basis. Ray and Angela had made some decisions in the guest area to accommodate his family's needs. They even referred to it as "Patrick's Place." The appropriateness of this did not go unnoticed since the Knowledge area reflects the energy around the youngest son as well.

I did express concern that the garage, Patrick's Place, was coming off the house at an angle which can set up frenzy. This may not reflect in Patrick's life because he would only be a visitor, but would most likely reflect in Ray and Angela's lives. The lot size did not permit them to "straighten out" the garage so I suggested they mark the spot where the garage would be if it had been built straight across. They had to imagine it could be swung around to be flush with the front of their house. On that spot (✳) they could plant a tree or a flag, possibly a bird bath. They were open to any number of suggestions.

However, when superimposing the bagua on this revised layout, they would be missing all of Wealth. They had clearly expressed concern about maintaining their wealth. In addition to marking where the garage would be, Ray and Angela would need to mark the furthermost corner to square off the space (◆).

The angle dilemma was also apparent in their eating area. The breakfast room had been built with angled walls to capture a view of the lake. Yet the feature sets up fast activity, not usually in a way that is welcome. I pointed out that they had built a lovely hint of an octagon in their master bedroom and suggested they change the breakfast area to mirror that shape. It would give a symmetry to their home, plus it wouldn't obstruct any views to the lake.

Their concern for health prompted some suggestions regarding their foyer. Having the dining room so close to the front entrance sets up digestive problems, not to mention reflecting a pattern of inadequate support when support is needed. People have a tendency to come to eat, but have a quick way out when so close to the front door. Additionally, there is a powder room on the other side of the foyer which is another digestive problem. The drain from the toilet takes away the occupants' health. In order to diminish both of those challenges, I suggested that the entrance to the dining room from the foyer either be walled in or have doors which could be closed. And I suggested that the door to the powder room would have to be kept closed as well.

The architect had positioned a bathroom toilet exactly behind the stove. It doesn't take a lot of imagination to realize that those two energies do not mix well. I suggested they move their stovetop to the island. Since they've used that partial octagon shape so often in the kitchen already, I strongly encouraged them to make the island an octagon also. Not only would the stovetop be away from the toilet, it would also enable the cook to get a better view of the entrance to the kitchen. Whether coming from the garage or the front door, people would not catch the cook off guard. Cooking with your back to entrances leaves the cook susceptible to surprises. This metaphor not only applies to cooking, but, on a bigger picture, to life in general.

In their bedroom, which was very auspiciously placed in the Partnership area of their space, we discussed the positioning of their bed. It seemed obvious to place it on the outside wall so they could have a view of their entrances as well as out the windows in the octagonal bay area.

Having the library by the front door is a good position for this room. It is a strong statement about the intellectual interests of Ray and Angela and leaves a good first impression.

Ray and Angela went back to their architect with the suggestions I had made. When I saw the final drawings (see *Final Plan),* they had incorporated all the proposed changes along with some additional ones of their own. The biggest change was that the garage was no longer situated at an angle. When I asked about this change, both Ray and Angela were quick to tell me the architect hadn't liked that feature all along. He didn't know exactly why, but was very happy to have an excuse to make a change. They still needed to adjust for a missing piece in the Wealth area (◆).

They closed off the opening to the dining room, creating a lighted alcove in the wall in which to display artwork. Upon reflection, Ray and Angela realized that they didn't need a formal dining room. They were quite certain it would never get used. So what had been the dining room became the laundry room and the powder room. They bought a table for the breakfast area that could be expanded to accommodate visitors as needed. This being their Wealth area, they decided that the more frequent use of this eating area would be beneficial.

The master bathroom had been re-configured to allow the powder room by the front door to sit further away from the foyer. A privacy wall had also been installed to insure no influence from the toilet would be possible. During the building process, I suggested that they drop nine Chinese coins in each of the corners of their house so that "wealth" would be built right into the walls of their new home.

Building a dream

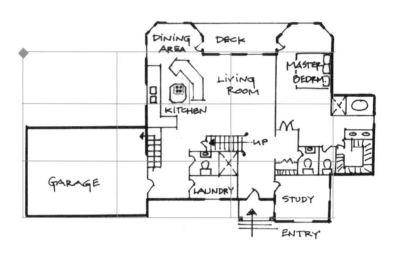

Final Plan

The house held a more balanced and more stable feel. Ray and Angela have been enjoying their space for several years now. As they had hoped, their children frequently return, filling their home with excitement and activity. Patrick's Place has been used not only by their own children, but also by one of Ray's brothers who needed a place to live while his life was in transition. Their health continues strong and steady as do their financial investments.

Jeff and Rita

Creating abundance

A dear friend called me to ask if I would help out a couple she knew from her church. The couple, Jeff and Rita, had fallen on some desperate times, had no money, and was forced to move into subsidized housing. My friend wanted to give them a Feng Shui appointment.

I'm always cautious about gift certificates because sometimes the recipient doesn't quite know what to do with a two-hour Feng Shui "gift." I asked if I could speak to Jeff or Rita first to get a feel for their interest in Feng Shui. A brief phone conversation with Rita allayed any concerns or hesitations I may have had about going to their apartment, so we set up a time.

Their apartment was on the fifth floor of an eight-story building. It was modestly, yet nicely, furnished, but I could see some challenging structural issues from the minute I walked in. When Rita opened the door to let me in, we had to do this awkward dance around the door. There was a blocking wall so intrusive to the entry space that there was no room to comfortably enter their apartment. She graciously took my coat and led me into the living room.

Jeff was not working due to a back condition that prevented him from doing his job as a construction worker. It was his intention to return to the work world, but he needed to do some kind of re-training of his skills first. Before that could happen, he had to get well. Rita had been laid off her job as a graphic artist due to lack of work. She was not computer literate so any future for her in this field would require additional schooling. Until they could afford that she was trying to pick up some temporary work. Added to this was an unpaid loan made a few years ago to a relative who clearly was not going to live up to the repayment plan. Their combined unemployment checks didn't meet their financial obligations, so they were forced to move into government subsidized housing to make ends meet.

One of the first things I wanted to look at was that wall by the entrance. The space was so tight the door just barely cleared the wall. Furthermore, when the door swung open, it aimed you towards the bathroom. If you wanted to get into the living room, you had to close the door first to get around it. Besides that, on the other side of the blocking wall was the mechanical/storage room. Their furnace was situated so it ended up in the Health area of their apartment. The restriction of the door was in the Career area.

Now these are challenges I've seen before so I quickly and auto-matically began to list off the common adjustments for a blocking wall, a door that opens the wrong way, a furnace in Health, etc., etc. What I wasn't expecting was their direct responses to me about each of the items I suggested—"We can't afford to do that." Jeff and Rita were very sincere in following the energetic flow of my Feng Shui logic, and they strongly wanted to get out of this spot, but they liter-ally had no money. Buying even the smallest mirror was not going to happen. I needed to re-group.

I explained to them the idea of a mirror on the blocking wall was to give a sense of space, so the wall didn't feel so close to the door. But perhaps they might have a painting, a poster, a picture of some-thing which had a dimensional feel to it? Something which would give the illusion of space? No, they didn't have anything like that. A travel poster? No, not that either. Rita said, "Gee, on my last job as a graphic artist, I hand painted a garden scene as a mural for a client. Too bad, I don't have a picture of that." I pounced. "Do you have some of your

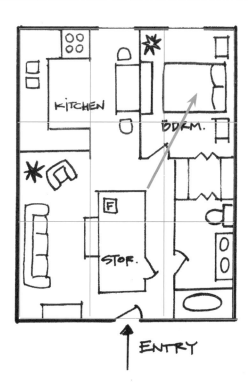

KITCHEN

BDRM.

F

STOR.

ENTRY

paints here?" "All of them, why?" Before I could answer, she figured it out—she could paint the garden scene right on the wall. Her eyes lit up. She began to describe the scene in great detail to Jeff—the birds, the fountain, a little bench. In their enthusiasm, I reminded them that their intention was to make "an opening" or "an expansion" for both of them to allow the energy of new and productive careers to enter their lives. I had to drag them away from the wall before I lost them in the excitement of the mural—there was a lot more to look at.

To avoid the energy from going "down the drain" in the bathroom, I suggested keeping the door to the bathroom closed. That wasn't going to work because there was no fan in there and they were both concerned that it would get stuffy. We agreed they would close the door partially to minimize the impact of the toilet, but let it be open wide enough to allow air circulation. The close proximity of the bathroom to the front door sets up the potential for health problems. It seemed to me they didn't need anything more like that in their lives.

Another health issue was having the furnace in the center of their space. The potential for "burn out" is high with this situation. Typically, you place a small mirror on the top of the furnace face down to keep the fire in check (mirrors being water elements). We had to get water in there in some other way without them having to purchase a mirror. As soon as I said "water" Jeff suggested that they set a bowl of water on the furnace; each day one of them could check it to see that the water hadn't dried up. Rita pulled out a ceramic bowl they had bought years ago at an art fair. The earth element of the bowl would also decrease the energy of the fiery furnace. They found a place to set it where it wouldn't get too hot and filled it up while I was still there.

Due to their situation, it seemed critical to look in their Wealth area for ways to enhance their income. This happened to be in the kitchen/dining area. All I needed to do was look at the condition of the kitchen to know there might be a problem in the area of making money. I couldn't help but wonder if all the apartments in this subsidized building were set up the same way, limiting people in career advancement, burning out their health, and now taking money from their lives. It made me wonder how any of these tenants would be able to get out of their situations and move ahead in life.

The kitchen was by far the most dilapidated part of their apartment. The cupboards needed painting, the linoleum on the floor was chipped, and the faucet was leaking. They had no response from the landlord about any of their requests to improve this area. I explained the metaphor about leaking money going down the drain just as the drips of water were draining away from the water tap.

Jeff decided he'd approach the landlord to provide some paint with which to paint the cupboards themselves. Since the cupboards were dark brown, he was going to see if he could paint them white to lighten up the kitchen. Rita was eager to explore the possibilities of painting some kind of designs on the cupboards. I explained the connection of the color purple with Wealth, so she promised she'd consider adding some purple to whatever she did. Jeff was quite sure his brother could fix the faucet for them. With regard to the lino-leum, Rita assured me they had a rug they could put over the flooring to minimize the impact of such an impoverished look. None of these things was difficult. They were kind of surprised at them-selves that it hadn't occurred to them before now to take care of matters on their own. By realizing that this area reflected the state of their money, fixing up what needed to be repaired became more imminent than it had before our talk.

The other issue in the kitchen was the stove. Two of the four burners didn't work. There's a story in Chinese history which con-nects money, food, and fire. If a person is cooking food over a fire, the implied message is that they had some money with which to get this food. The more fires, the more food, therefore, the more money. When burners don't work on a stove, there is money potential being missed. Again, requests to the landlord to get this repaired had fallen on deaf ears.

I knew I'd have to work with something they already owned, so I asked if they had a stainless steel kettle, or teapot, or a bowl—a wok? No to all these. I was looking for something reflective they could place on one of the burners which didn't work to reflect the ones which did. Jeff reminded her of a matching set of candy dishes they had received as a wedding gift years ago. It didn't take Rita long to locate the two round bowls that had been carefully packed away. She seemed reticent to set these two beautiful and expensive bowls on the stove where they could get spattered and dirty.

Jeff's common sense reminded her that they weren't being appreciated where they were, so why not bring them out? They could be a reminder to them of vessels with which they could gather their money. He took it further by suggesting they put change in the bowls to begin money flowing. Rita was less than enthusiastic about the idea, but agreed to try setting one bowl on each of the non-working burners.

What also would happen with those bowls is that when Jeff or Rita was standing at the stove, they could look in the reflection of the bowl or bowls to detect anyone coming up from behind to catch them off guard.

They didn't have much cupboard space in this little kitchen, so the countertops were pretty cluttered. I explained to them the direct correlation between horizontal spaces and creativity. Both aspects relate to "vision," both literally and figuratively. The more cluttered their countertops, the more restricted their vision. Jeff and Rita reacted with horror at the condition of their creative energy. Rita began picking up various items declaring "we don't need this" or "this is no good anymore" or "let's throw these out." Within two minutes a huge area had been cleared off the counters. I didn't want her to get involved in doing a massive cleaning job just then, but I assured her she had the idea!

I wanted to show them a poison arrow aiming right at the entrance to their bedroom. This feature was the result of the storage area in the center of their space. It was virtually thrusting energy quickly and strongly, not only into their bedroom, but also onto their bed. Both Jeff and Rita assured me they each experienced restless nights. They attributed it to their worries about their future. A poison arrow, however, can greatly exacerbate a situation. Keeping the door closed at night kept either the heat out in the winter or the air conditioning out in the summer. There was not enough room to set something in front of the corner to take the brunt of its "edge"-iness as the hall was narrow as it was. Setting something there like a plant would be in the way and most likely get knocked over.

The wall went all the way to the ceiling so there was no ledge on which to set a trailing plant to vine its way down and over the corner.

Rita asked about fabric. Fabric? "What if I draped some fabric over the corner, bunching it at the top and having it drape down to the floor?" I had a hard time getting a visual on this, but she seemed to have something in mind. She had some sheer off-white panels she had saved to use someday.

I left them for now. We all decided that working on the front wall by the entrance would be critical to get things going for them. This would be the place for them to begin.

Four to five months passed. Jeff called me one day announcing that they were moving! He asked if I'd like to come and see what they'd done before they vacated their space. I couldn't wait to see their apartment and to hear their story.

Jeff had finished his computer training and had been hired by a company to begin the day after he graduated. The money was good and the potential was even better. Rita had been given some freelance illustration work from her past employer which paid her well. Meanwhile, they furiously worked on their apartment.

The biggest change was the experience coming into their place. Rita had outdone herself. The mural she had painted on the blocking wall was exquisite and breathtaking. It looked as though you could walk though an archway into a garden and down a flower-lined path.

You could tell she was proud of her work. The landlord had found it so charming he asked that they leave it for the next tenant. I was still not prepared for what was to come.

They took me into their kitchen where I stood speechless. They had indeed painted their cupboards white. The landlord supplied them with all the materials they needed to do it right—primer, sanding equipment, paint, etc. The cupboards looked like a professional had done them. Rita painted the handles a very pale lavender and had added small lavender and green pinstripes around the edge of each cupboard. The landlord was so impressed with what they were doing that he offered to provide them some linoleum squares to replace their flooring. With new white tiles and white cupboards, the place looked twice its size. Rita had made a lavender tablecloth for their table. I couldn't help but notice the faucet wasn't dripping and their silver bowls were overflowing with change!

Jeff and Rita were moving from here to a townhouse, renting with an option to buy. Slowly, but surely, they were getting themselves out of debt. They projected that they would be able to purchase the townhouse within eighteen months. Yet they admitted they had come to love their space and even had some regrets about leaving.

Not all things were resolved. Although they were sleeping better, Jeff was still having back trouble and experiencing sleepless nights.

They never did get the money owed them from their relative, despite repeated attempts. Most importantly, however, they were able to move up and out of a space that, due to its patterns, continuously fed them a message of being blocked and penniless.

Jennifer

Matching goals to a space

Jennifer called me to look at a couple of house plans for a small home she was planning to build in the next few months. The house was part of a development, so she would be limited in making any substantial deviations from the blueprints. Each house design was one story with an unfinished basement where the laundry would be located. Both of them also had detached garages. Jennifer was trying to decide which one would be the better choice for her.

Jennifer and I sat and chatted for a while about what she was looking for in the next few years. This was her first house and, because of its size, she didn't expect to live there for years and years.

It was her intention to meet someone, get married, and start a family in the near future. She also wanted to make some changes in her career as a computer software analyst to get into a company which would pay her more money. Also, a big issue for her was health, as she had been diagnosed with clinical depression a couple of years prior. This was a continual struggle for Jennifer despite the fact that she was doing many things to counteract it.

We looked at House A first to see what might be a challenge and what would be a blessing for her. I liked that the master bedroom was in the Partnership area. It's very powerful when a room matches the energy of that area. Having a study close to the front door wasn't a problem. Jennifer was planning to decorate it so it looked like a study, but would have a foldout couch so guests would have a place to stay.

The Health area had challenging features in the plan of House A, with the powder room in the center and the stairs going down to the basement. The toilet, sink, and bathtub are "draining" to health and the stairway sends a message of having an "up and down" status with health. Not only that, the eating area was very close to the front door allowing the nutrition of food to be overwhelmed by the energy coming in through the door as well as enabling any good nutrition to escape, depriving the occupants of good health.

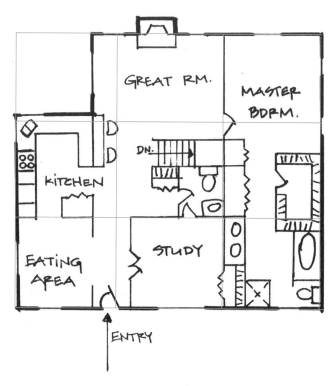

GREAT RM.

MASTER BDRM.

KITCHEN

DN.

EATING AREA

STUDY

ENTRY

House A

Jennifer would have a missing piece in the Wealth area since that corner was currently designed as just a patio. To qualify to be part of the bagua, the area must have a roof and sides, which a patio does not have. She had been thinking of having the builder enclose it, making it a three-season porch. Because of our discussion, perhaps she would enclose the patio and have it be her eating area. This would move the eating area away from close proximity to the front of the house. She could create a seating area near the front, even a small library. This would be a very welcome invitation to those coming in through her front door.

House B was not without some challenges as well. Having the master bedroom in the front of the house is not restful nor does it enable the owner of the house to make a strong claim to the space. The second bedroom was considerably smaller, so it wouldn't be a good option to simply have Jennifer sleep in the back bedroom and leave the original master bedroom as a guest room. The stairs going down to the basement were very evident when entering the space. She felt it would be possible to turn the stairs to descend from the other end.

Once again, the eating area was designated close to the front door. In fact, a table would probably be in front of the line of the front door. Both of these features relate to health issues. Both plans had the fireplace in the Fame and Reputation area which is very positive. The

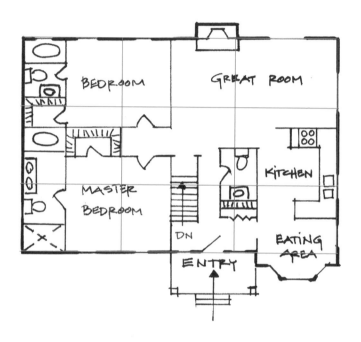

BEDROOM

GREAT ROOM

MASTER BEDROOM

KITCHEN

DN

ENTRY

EATING AREA

House B

fire from the fireplace matches the fire represented by Fame and Reputation.

Jennifer decided to work with House A to see if she could eliminate the missing piece. I thought she had done a nice job of incorporating the things we had discussed (see *House A-1*). The new layout also gave her a few more square feet of living space.

The house was built in July. During the building process, I had Jennifer drop a small toy boat in the wall near her front door to represent "her ship coming in." By September she was in a new job which gave her the potential of doubling her income. The study in her new house was quickly transformed into an office before the builder was done because this new job would enable her to work part of the time from her home.

She met a man in December at a Christmas party who became her husband the following summer. They currently live in the house together, but are searching for a much larger one to buy together. Jennifer continues to struggle with depression, but with the new, exciting things happening to her, she is better able to cope. When I last spoke to her, they had put their moving plans on hold as she was pregnant with their first child. She and her husband were waiting to move until after the baby was born.

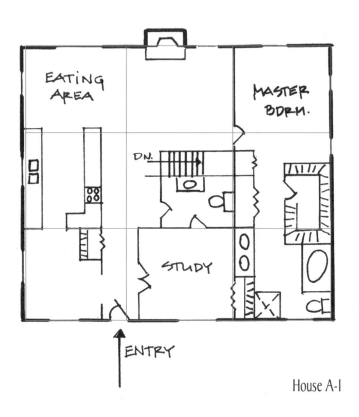

House A-1

Abby

Expanding life in a small space

Before I knocked on Abby's apartment door, I
noticed a slight tightening of the muscles in my
back. The sounds of crying and shouting children was emanating
from somewhere. I looked around, hoping it was coming from
another apartment. But when she opened the door, I took a breath as
the screams blew over me in high decibel range.

Abby seemed flustered at the behavior of her children and apolo-
gized for the disruption. She was a single mother, raising a three- and
a five-year-old in a two-bedroom apartment. She spent the first five
minutes I was there getting the five-year-old (Jason) settled with a

video and the three-year-old (Joey) with some juice and crackers. I was soon to learn that would only last about ten minutes.

Her apartment was filled with kid things—toys, trikes, a small table and chairs. The furniture showed the typical wear and tear from having active children around. The breakfast dishes were still on the table. Both boys were in their pajamas although it was nearly 11:00 AM. Abby, looking tired, was in sweat pants and a sweat shirt. She was clearly overwhelmed. I asked her if this was an appropriate time to do this appointment. Maybe she'd want to re-schedule? She felt confident the boys would settle down, so we began.

A couple minutes into our discussion on Feng Shui, she had to get up to fix the video for Jason as it wasn't working properly. More discussion. Joey then spilled his juice all over the table and himself as well. After she got him into a new outfit and cleaned up the mess, we began again. In between, she would jump up and down to keep turning the volume down on the video, which Jason would promptly turn back up to a loud level. While Abby would tend to her children, I had an opportunity to take in the surroundings. She had a lot of furniture in this small apartment—more than what was comfortable. She shared with me that people would continue to give her things— chairs, tables, lamps. She didn't have the heart to tell them no.

Despite the interruptions, Abby wanted more than anything to get help with her life and her boys. They had moved here after her divorce. She worked part time to bring in a little income, but mostly they relied on child support from her ex-husband. Meanwhile, her ex-husband had moved out of state, so he saw the boys only briefly each summer, which left Abby no respite from the constant needs of two small children. In addition, Jason, her older son, had allergies and her younger, Joey, had just been tested for ADD. Each one of them required time and energy she didn't have.

Not only did she want some help with her feelings of being overwhelmed, but she needed money and better health for her children and herself. A partner would be nice, but it seemed too far fetched to think someone would be interested in her at this point in her life.

Before we began walking through the apartment together, Abby had to find some other form of entertainment for the boys. Jason was bored with the video. Joey was bored with Jason. She found them some coloring books and crayons and set them up at their little table. We seemed to have a brief reprieve. She explained to me that she had asked someone to take them for a couple hours during our appointment, but the sitter had called the night before saying she was sick and wouldn't be able to help her. She couldn't find anyone else at the last minute, so she was hoping they would find some way to entertain themselves while I was there.

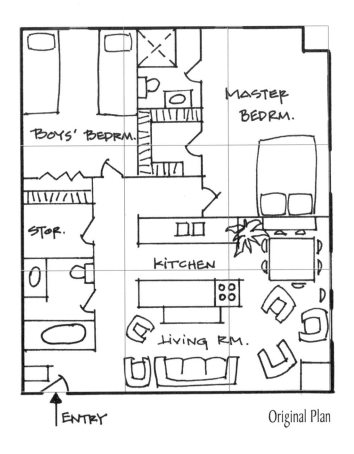

BOYS' BEDRM.

MASTER
BEDRM.

STOR.

KITCHEN

Living RM.

ENTRY

Original Plan

One of the first issues I wanted to address with Abby was her front door (see *Original Plan*). For some reason she had moved a file cabinet behind the door. Whenever the door was opened, it only opened half way. Her explanation was that it was the only place she could find to store it. Having her door only open half way was limiting her possibilities and opportunities. I almost didn't care where she put that cabinet, just not behind her front door. She seemed daunted by that first recommendation. It had been a huge undertaking to move the cabinet there in the first place. I couldn't state strongly enough, that it had to be removed. She needed her door to swing wide and welcome in all the good luck she could find.

On top of that, she had a blocked entry because the bathroom wall faced the front door head-on. I suggested a mirror be hung there(-)

When we moved into the living room, after soothing a screaming match between the two boys, Abby remarked that she wished she could afford new furniture. She didn't like the way the room looked and was sure new furniture would solve the issue. In response to my question about how much she entertained or how many people came to visit, she assured me that she didn't invite too many people into the apartment—perhaps her parents, or her sister once in a while. I suggested she remove half the chairs she had. They were crowding her living room, nobody sat in most of them, and for the most part they weren't all that attractive and none of them matched.

The dilemma for Abby was that well-meaning people had given them to her to help her out. By getting rid of them, she felt she'd be ungrateful. We decided there might be space for one of the chairs in her bedroom and possibly one of them in her boys' room. At this suggestion, her older boy overheard us and reacted vehemently about any changes in his room. She suggested to Jason that if there were a chair in his room, she could read stories to him in that chair. He still didn't take to that well, so we assured him there would be no changes unless he wanted them. It took several minutes for him to settle down. Abby took him into his room, found a new coloring book and a new box of crayons which he threw back at her. She decided to try to carry him around with us.

In the dining room, I suggested simply removing a leaf of the table to give them more floor space. It wouldn't seem so crowded with a smaller table and fewer chairs. To enhance the Children and Creativity area of her apartment, I suggested she place pictures of her and her two boys on the china cabinet she had in the eating area. It would require a major re-shifting of assorted dishes, books, and miscellaneous items that were currently sitting there. Amidst answering Jason's questions and tending to his needs, Abby agreed that the cabinet needed care, but couldn't imagine when she'd get enough time to do it. There was also an oversized plant alongside the cabinet which required a person to duck when entering the kitchen. That would need to be moved to open up to an easier flow of the energy in her space.

Her face began to look overwhelmed and confused. The boys were getting on edge. We were only one hour into the appointment. I suggested that I leave and come back later. She had some things to work on for now. She jumped at the suggestion. We both breathed a sigh of relief as I headed out the door.

Two weeks later I returned to Abby's apartment. The boys were off with their grandmother for the day. Abby looked like an entirely new person. So did her living room (see *Final Plan*). I didn't even ask where all the chairs went. I only cared that they were gone. She had managed to work in an intimate little conversation area around the sofa, had reduced the size of the dining table, and moved the plant. The cabinet was better, but still needed some work. And she hadn't yet found a place for the file cabinet that was so steadfastly preventing her door from opening all the way. Nevertheless, she could tell herself that the differences were already huge. This time I knew we'd be able to make some headway.

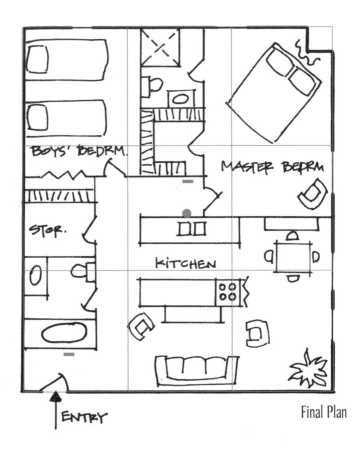

BOYS' BEDRM.

MASTER BEDRM

STOR.

KITCHEN

ENTRY

Final Plan

We spent a fair amount of time in her bedroom. I wanted her to move her bed out of the doorway. She told us that she didn't sleep well, but wanted to be close to her boys' room. I suggested that she move the bed into the back corner where it would be in a stronger position and more stable for her. A power position is the back corner furthest from the entrance. From the power position, Abby could feel like she's more in control of her life. She had a small missing piece in the Wealth area of that room, and I thought we could do a couple of adjustments at once. I suggested she move her bed into that corner at a diagonal, since the room was big enough to do so, and drape some fabric down from the ceiling to the back of her bed to conceal the corner. A corner like this produces a poison arrow, creating aggressive and confrontive energy. It's hard to sleep in the energy of something like that unless some measures are taken to disguise it. Likewise, the fabric could make it seem as though the missing piece was not missing at all. Additionally, Abby didn't have a headboard, so the fabric could create a sense of backing and support. She assured me she loved the idea and would get on it right away.

In the master bathroom, the mirror above the sink was small and cracked. Each morning she would have to stoop to look in the mirror and each morning the reflection was telling her she wasn't whole. Abby was aghast at the thought of such a message. She had a bigger mirror somewhere in her storage closet which she promised she'd find for that wall.

I also wanted to find the center of her apartment where the Health area was located. The exact center was in the hall, a couple of feet in front of her bedroom door. She agreed to hang a round, faceted crystal from the ceiling to mark this spot (●). If there was one place in which she could facilitate some harmony and balance in her life, this would be a very strong place in which to do so. The intention of well-being could affect not only her own life, but that of her children.

The boys' room also needed to have the beds moved. Jason, the older son, was sleeping in the doorway, with his feet pointing out the door and down the hall which is a health challenge. He was also sleeping on a wall shared by a toilet which is another health challenge. I suggested that both beds be moved to the other side of the room so both boys could see the door, but not be in the doorway.

In the kitchen, the biggest issue was the stove being on the end of the countertop with its side being exposed to the eating area. Her younger son had nearly burned himself severely when he ran by the side of the stove, hit a pot handle, and dumped boiling potatoes all over the kitchen. Abby decided to put a screen alongside the stove to protect her kids and keep the stovetop enclosed.

Another issue was the stovetop in the front half of the house. What this situation can create is an imbalance in the Health area of a person's life. The kitchen itself should be toward the back part of the house or apartment. Since moving the kitchen was not an option, I suggested a full-length mirror on the wall in the hallway leading into her bedroom. This mirror would reflect and "move" the kitchen wall into the back half of her apartment. Additionally, I always suggest that there be a full-length mirror somewhere in the space, to reflect a total and complete image of who you are. This mirror could do both jobs.

A few months later, Abby asked if I would like to stop by to see her apartment. It was summer and her boys were with their father for a couple weeks. I ran in quickly on my way to another appointment. The changes in her apartment weren't nearly as spectacular as the changes in Abby's life and demeanor. Although the boys were still a handful, she had gotten some issues resolved around Jason's neediness and anger. She was working with a preschool psychologist and they were getting some great results. Jason was sleeping better and was becoming a big brother to Joey, by helping him dress and clean up his toys.

After such a short time of doing Feng Shui adjustments, Abby was quick to tell me how she loved her apartment. She was considering a long-term stay in the space, something she had never considered before. As long as the boys were young enough and could continue to share a room, there was no need to think about moving them. There was no new partner in her life, but she seemed indifferent about that issue anyway. She had moved her bed and was sleeping well. Being rested meant a world of difference for her. Her patience and centeredness were rubbing off on her boys.

What she hadn't shared with me during our previous appointments was that she had been on medication for depression for the last year. She was now feeling strong enough to begin the gradual process of getting off the drug. Abby was starting to feel whole again.

Marty

An office on the move

Marty got my name from a local newspaper article he had read. He was divi-
sion president of a major corporation in the city and they were about
to move into new headquarters. A frequent visitor to Hong Kong,
Marty knew the importance of Feng Shui in his business dealings
there, so he decided to have someone check out their new building.
To avoid suspicion among his supervisors and staff, he had decided to
pay for the consultation himself.

   We set up a time to meet at the new building. It was still under
construction but the walls would be going up soon. He thought this

would be a good time to have some input about positioning of certain staff and size of offices. He made it clear to me on the phone that he wanted to have this appointment privately with me and he expressed more than once the importance of confidentiality.

You can imagine my surprise when I showed up at the site met by Marty and five other people. His secretary Lisa got wind of the appointment and asked to come along. As the word spread a man from engineering asked to come along as well, then one of the vice presidents and finally two people from building maintenance. They all assured me that they had come along to listen. Within 10 minutes I could tell this was not a listening bunch of people. Each one had their own agenda, wanting me to look in their own potential offices or cubicles, hoping I'd give them the advice they'd need to change their lives.

I kept checking in with Marty to see if he wanted me to be handling this some other way. After all, he was paying for this appointment. He had evidently resigned himself to the direction this was going. He graciously and generously allowed each of them some time with me. In fact, he even wandered off looking at the progression of other areas of the construction. When his secretary Lisa and I began discussing the placement of her office, however, it was imperative that Marty become involved in the conversation because it was going to affect his office choice.

It seems Marty had intended to move into an office near the front entrance. He was very much a people person and wanted to be involved in the comings and goings that occur near the front desk. He figured it would be handy for the many people who came to see him—they wouldn't have to walk very far to his office. Lisa would also be stationed near the front since she was his executive secretary, where she, too, could easily be drawn into the hectic frenzy near the reception desk.

I explained to Marty that, as the leader, as the president, as the visionary, he needed to take an anchor spot in the space. He needed to be in a strong driving position to lead this huge division to success and profitability. This command position was not in the front of the office, but in the back corner furthest from the front entrance. The back office I was suggesting according to the layout was a corner one, giving Marty vision in many directions, both in reality and in metaphor. It was one of the biggest offices which seemed appropriate for him given his title. Marty was planning on making it a conference room for that very reason—it was the biggest room.

All five people were rapt with attention as we discussed Marty's position in the company. He still opted to be near the front, however. From a Feng Shui perspective, anyone situated near the front entrance of a business, unless they're sales people, tends not to stay around.

An office on the move

The energy of the coming and going activity that naturally occurs in a reception area can sweep away anyone nearby. This is why receptionist positions can have a high rate of turnover. Remembering how Marty wanted this appointment to be private, I couldn't bring myself to say this to him in front of the five extra pair of ears.

Without saying the exact words, I tried to impress on Marty the importance of being in the back of the office. At times, I must have seemed adamant. I finally decided I'd just call him and have a private conversation about the matter. I suggested a phone follow-up in a couple days and, although open to it, he informed me that he would be leaving on extensive business travel in two days and would be gone almost until their move-in date. I stressed that I would still contact him before he left. He was fine with that.

I called three different times. Each time Lisa graciously took the message, assured me she was giving him his messages, but also assured me that Marty was extremely busy. In her friendly way, appropriate to her position, she insisted that if I just shared with her the reason for my call, she might be able to act as a liaison. Of course, I wasn't going to share my concerns: "Look, Lisa, your boss is sitting too close to the door. It's possible that he's either going to quit or he might get fired." Marty left on his travels and we never had a chance to speak to one another.

Four months after our appointment, a casual glance through the morning newspaper presented some astounding news, although not surprising. The business section's lead story was about Marty's company. A lot of internal upheaval had come to a head resulting in the unexpected resignation by one of the presidents—Marty. He had occupied his new office exactly one month before leaving abruptly.

A week after the news article, Marty left a message for me on my voice mail. When he and I finally connected, he let me know he was starting his own company and wanted some advice. I met him again, this time under totally different circumstances. For one thing, we were alone. This time his office was small and efficient for he was beginning a new endeavor with one other person.

He admitted that he knew during our original appointment that I had picked up some issue about his decision to leave. He had been planning to resign for over a year, but, once he got into the new building, it happened quicker than he had expected. Marty confessed that if the other staff had not been present, he and I might have had a totally different experience. Although he regretted the outcome of our appointment together, he also knew that things had unfolded as they should.

His new office was on a whole new scale, being smaller in size and in staff. Marty was the majority partner, so we selected the office that was in the command position for him. We made sure he had room to position a desk so that he would be facing the entry door to the office. The one issue that was occurring in this new space was that he was on the 15th floor of a large office building. Each of the offices had floor to ceiling windows, providing no support for the people trying to work there. I had just suggested placing his desk in such a way that Marty would have his back to these windows. We needed to make sure he could pull his desk forward enough so he could have either a credenza behind him as he sat at his desk or at least some tall plants to provide a wall of security. A credenza seemed to be the most practical for Marty.

By placing him in the command position of the space, Marty wound up being right next door to the public bathrooms. Although he wasn't sharing a wall with any of the toilets or urinals, he was afraid he'd be bothered by the sound of all the flushing. I suggested a fountain be brought into his office to provide some soothing, background sounds. The bubbling of a fountain could mask the bathroom noises enough so that he wouldn't be distracted by them. Besides, a fountain would symbolize the flow of money in his new business venture.

In the initial start of the partnership, Marty confirmed that they were not going to hire a receptionist until it was absolutely warranted. I wondered how he would know whether anyone had walked in through the front door since his new office and that of his partner were visually removed from the line of sight of the entrance. Marty figured the two of them would just listen for the door opening and whoever wasn't tied up on the phone or involved with another client would get up and greet the visitor. The problem with that theory, I assured them, was that the space was carpeted which muffled any sound and the door opened silently. They would both have to visually check the reception area on a regular basis in case anyone had walked in, which would require them to get up and walk out into the hallway. Marty didn't like the idea of a bell on the door as it reminded him of a little retail shop. He thought he might like a buzzer of some sort. I encouraged him to make sure the buzzer was pleasant and not startling. He would want to walk out to meet someone with a smile on his face, not a startled look of annoyance.

Marty discussed a carpet color with me, since the existing carpet was going to be replaced by the management of the building. Based on the Chinese Five Elements theory, Marty's tall height and pioneering spirit assured me that his wood element was in high gear. To support his new business, I suggested a gray or green color (gray is a water color, which would support his wood; green is a wood color, which would add to his natural element). I also suggested he purchase, as an abundance adjustment, three, six, or nine Chinese coins and place them on the floor before the new carpet was being laid. The coins would be most effective being placed near the entrance to their space. This theme of financial success would be energetically present the moment someone walked in.

Marty proudly showed me their new logo, which was modern, sleek and encased in a circular shape. It was very indicative of the cutting edge business he was creating. I suggested that they might want to cut the design into the carpet in the center of their space. The center was in a hallway, not far from the front entrance. He totally resonated with this idea. He figured that if they moved on to another place, they could patch in a piece of carpet so the successive tenants would never know. I assured him that placing a round shape near the center would help to bring balance and harmony to his new business. After all the turmoil of his past experience, balance and harmony sounded refreshing to Marty.

I also suggested that, if possible, Marty and his partner incorporate the five colors associated with the Five Elements in the reception area—red, yellow, black, white and green. When all five colors are used within a space, there is an automatic sense of balance and unity. We figured that if Marty chose gray carpet (black), moved in a couple of large plants (green), used wood furnishings (tan/yellow), then they could accent with red and white. Red flowers in a reception area is desirable to keep the energy moving. He liked that idea. He also decided that he could keep the walls a white or off-white to bring the final element color into play.

We selected an auspicious date for him to open his business based on Chinese astrology. I left him that day, having had quite a different experience from our first appointment. His business far surpassed his expectations. Within a year Marty had to move to bigger offices and had expanded his staff to six. Along the way, he's been careful to keep himself in the driver's seat by locating his office in a back corner. An outdoorsman at heart, he mentioned to me that being in the back of his space makes sense to him for, like paddling a canoe, the steering must come from the back.

Denise

Re-defining a bedroom

After a series of classes and workshops, I had come to know Denise very well. For a time, her smiling face seemed to always appear in the front row. She was like a sponge taking in as much information as she could. She was remodeling she kept telling me. One day, however, she called me. "I'm stuck," she sighed. "I've done a lot of Feng Shui in my house, but something is still not right. I'd like an outside opinion."

We set up a time for me to visit her charming and quaint two-story home. She was on a corner lot with a detached garage. Denise was a woman who loved to garden which was evident from her yard, particularly from what she had created on the walkway between the garage and the back door. Her husband had divorced her three years earlier, an event around which she still held some sadness. A year after that, she had inherited a very large sum of money which enabled her to quit her job and begin an extensive remodeling project on her house. But, despite all the work, she was feeling as though something wasn't right.

By her front door, Denise had a blocked entry created by the front hall closet. However, she had hung a mirror on the front of the closet door. When she opened the closet itself, I must admit I saw the most beautiful closet I have ever seen. She had wallpapered the inside walls, hung a clever little chandelier inside, and installed wire shelving. She had installed brass hooks on which to hang her wide assortment of gardening hats, yet still had a small area to hang coats. It was a remarkable use of a small closet.

About six months before, Denise had redone her kitchen, incorporating lighter cabinets to replace the dark wood veneer ones typical of a house built in the '60s. Because she lived alone, she ate at a small 24-inch round glass table with two wire chairs by a window overlooking her backyard. If she had company, she'd use her larger dining room table. She had incorporated small 4-by-4-inch mirrors in the tile work on the backsplash in the kitchen. Denise had appropriately placed a couple of these little mirrors behind the stove to reflect the burners and to enable her to see movement behind her. She had also scattered a few on the wall where the missing piece in the Partnership area was located (see *Main Floor–Original Plan*). A drop ceiling with fluorescent lighting and ceiling panels had been removed, creating an expansive difference for her. The kitchen was one of her favorite rooms, she said.

Her bedroom was in the Wealth area of the house. This was the bedroom she and her ex-husband had shared. She didn't like the room, because it reminded her of him, though she had already repainted everything. The furniture was new and the arrangement was different than when they shared the space. Yet there was still something she didn't like about it.

On the second floor (see *Second Floor–Original Plan*), there was a guest room and a home office for her to pay bills and do correspondence. Both rooms had been re-wallpapered; both had beautiful dormer windows with window seats. Denise loved being up there and would often sleep in the guest room. When I suggested actually moving the master bedroom up there, she strongly resisted, as there was no bathroom up there. I said no more about the idea. We stood in the current master bedroom while I watched Denise struggle with everything I suggested. She no longer even knew if she liked the changes she had recently made to the room. All she could repeat was how it didn't feel right. I also couldn't help but observe how her face

Denise

MASTER BDRM.

UP

DN.

KITCHEN

PORCH

LIVING ROOM

ENTRY

Main Floor–Original Plan

Re-defining a bedroom

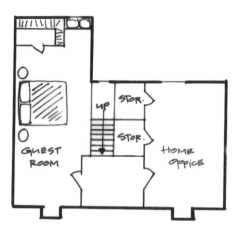

Second Floor–Original Plan

changed when we went back upstairs. She loved everything about that space. Offhandedly, she said that she probably could bring plumbing upstairs above the current master bath. I knew that would be expensive and didn't know if she would want to spend her money on such a project. I refrained from saying any more. It was only a moment or two when she realized the view of the garden out a bathroom on that floor would be spectacular. She spent a moment imagining what it would be like when she was taking her morning bath or brushing her teeth. The view from this floor was much better than on the first floor. I refrained again.

She told me that the bed in the guest room had a newer mattress and that was why she thought she slept better there. I refrained from even hinting about moving upstairs. Denise's favorite colors were blues which, of course, were the dominating colors in the guest room. I refrained again. She admitted that she felt safer upstairs than downstairs. Refrained.

She could make the lower master bedroom into a den for the television, currently in the basement, her least favorite spot in the house. If she did that, she could possibly incorporate a piano which she didn't have room for now. She'd really love that as she used to play the piano as a young girl and had been wanting to get back into playing . . . etc., etc., etc. Refrained again.

Re-defining a bedroom

We went back down to the master bedroom. Denise walked in with new eyes, envisioning the television and a piano in the room. She scrutinized where things might fit. I let her scrutinize and finally could no longer refrain.

Why not? I asked. I sensed her wrestling with questions: Is it all right to make a bedroom something else? Aren't there rules about doing something like that? What if I don't like it? She finally looked at me and said, "That's it. It can't be worse than where I am now."

I felt as though that might be all she needed from me for now. Denise called me with questions and confirmations several times during the process of changing things. She gave herself permission to begin sleeping upstairs that first night.

Six months later, I was at Denise's neighbors' home. In her enthusiasm and excitement, Denise had told them her story. One of them hired me to come and look at their home. After the appointment, I walked over to Denise's. I heard the tinkling of a piano as I approached her door. She was ecstatic showing me her "new house" (see *Main Floor–Revised Plan*) as she called it. The new den had taken shape very quickly. She had purchased an alcohol-burning fireplace for the den which requires no ventilation. The small upright piano fit

Denise

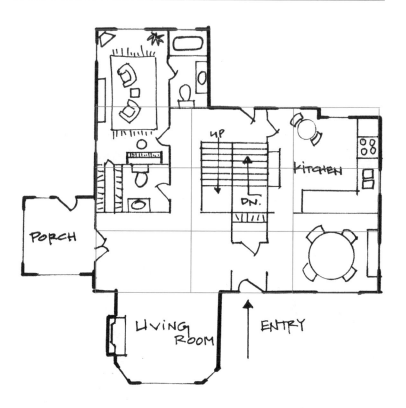

KITCHEN

UP

DN.

PORCH

LIVING ROOM

ENTRY

Main Floor–Revised Plan

beautifully in the corner. Denise had changed the entrance door to a French door since she didn't need the privacy anymore.

The new bathroom on the second floor (see *Second Floor–Revised Plan*) was done in impeccable style. I expected nothing less from Denise. She had worked in her favorite blue colors. Once the decision had been made, she admitted, it felt right. She never doubted the end result. She was convinced that the financial investment she had made to do all this remodeling would not only pay off for her when she sold her house, but it was already paying off for her by the energy shift in the space. She absolutely loved the den and adored her upstairs bedroom.

It is not unusual to be stuck in your own space and be unable to see an option. A new pair of eyes can often expand your outlook. I couldn't leave that day before Denise played "Blue Moon" on her piano.

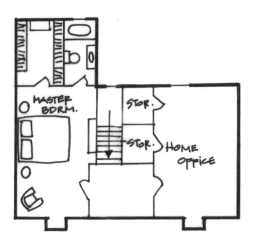

Second Floor–Final Plan

Mike and Julie

What happened to our marriage?

Mike was the one who actually called me about coming to his small home to assess the Feng Shui of the space. He and his wife Julie had been married for three years. A year ago they had bought their starter house, moved in, and watched their relationship disintegrate day by day. They were working with a marriage therapist and had attended a couple of marriage encounter groups. Still something wasn't right. They were thinking of moving out of the house just to save their marriage.

I could see the look of desperation and exhaustion on their faces when we met. They didn't know a lot about Feng Shui but couldn't explain the sudden shift in their relationship other than the possibility that something was wrong with the house. Before we began walking around, I sat with them and asked questions about the predecessors of the house. Their home was built in the '70s, so I figured there had to have been a few owners prior to Mike and Julie.

The first thing that Julie mentioned was that they had bought the house from a couple who was in a process of getting divorced. They had some interesting events during the closing on the house with the two estranged spouses sitting next to each other, bickering about endless details. That couple had lived in the space for five years.

I asked about other owners. They had heard from neighbors that, before their predecessors, there was a family who lived in the house about ten years. The wife had died unexpectedly one day, leaving a husband and two small children. Further, the original owners, who built the house, had lived in it for seven years before divorcing. Mike and Julie were shocked when they realized the divisive pattern was repeating itself. They had walked into a situation unsuspectingly and the pattern was beginning to play itself out in their own lives.

Obviously, the first thing I suggested was that we take a look in the Partnership area to see if anything seemed unusual (see *Main Floor– Original Plan*). I had spent time with them discussing the layout of the bagua based on the front door, delineating what the various areas rep-

What happened to our marriage?

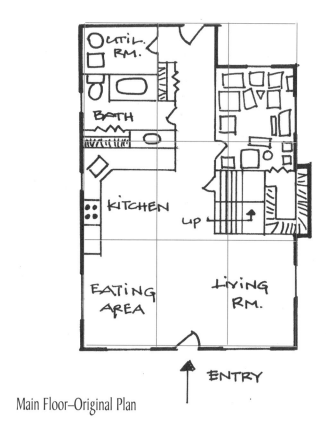

Main Floor–Original Plan

resented, and where the areas fell in their house. Before physically moving to the Partnership area, I could see from the blueprint that there was a missing piece located in that part of the house.

When we got to the room which held most of the Partnership energy, the door was closed. Mike said, "You're not going to have to go in there, are you?" Well, the idea was for me to look around the house, and I assured them I would have to open the door. Julie told it like it was: "It's our junk room!" Sure enough. When I opened the door, I could only get it partially open; boxes and miscellaneous stuff were piled from floor to ceiling. They had no basement in this house, and this became their storage area. Storage was one thing, this was something else.

I listened to their words as they talked about this room. "It's a mess." "I hate going in there." "It scares me to think about working in that area." "It's out of control." "It's mostly useless junk we can't seem to throw away." These were similar if not exact words they had both used in describing their marriage earlier in the appointment. It didn't take them long to realize that the principle *Your space mirrors your life* was applying directly to their relationship. My first advice was to clean out the room.

I also suggested that, when they got the Partnership room cleaned out, they hang a mirror on one of the walls of the missing area. It

What happened to our marriage?

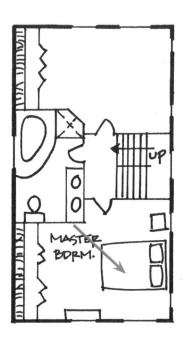

Upper Floor–Original Plan

would necessitate that they deal with the stuff in that area first in order to get a mirror incorporated. By simply hanging a mirror now with all the "junk" in the room, they would only succeed in doubling the junk.

When working on a relationship, making changes in the master bedroom is also appropriate, even when the master bedroom is not in the Partnership area. We spent a good deal of time in their bedroom discussing possible options (see *Upper Floor–Original Plan*). One of the main issues was that they had no headboard, which implies no support for one another. They also had one nightstand on one side of the bed. I advised two matching or similar nightstands with lamps to symbolize equality in their relationship. They also had adorned their bedroom walls with pictures of family members, parents, and grandparents. In the bedroom, pictures of Mike and/or Julie are the only images that should be present. The invasion of other people's energy diminishes the energy of an intimate partnership.

Neither Mike nor Julie had been sleeping well since they moved in, contributing to the short-tempered outbreaks which occurred between them. Even though the front bedroom was bigger, I suggested they move to the back bedroom, or at least give it a try. Being in the back of the house would afford them more privacy and possibly less noise from the street. I was also concerned about the

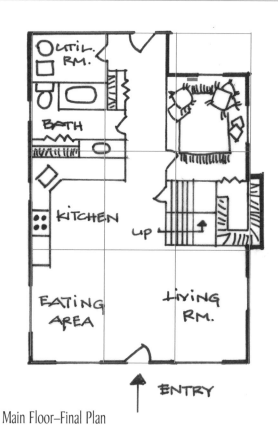

Main Floor–Final Plan

poison arrow coming from a corner by the entrance to the bedroom. The energy from that corner was shooting across the room and onto the bed. The back bedroom avoided that issue. Mike and Julie said they'd consider such a move. In the meantime, they could work on getting a headboard and nightstands.

Two months later, Julie called to say she was sending pictures of the Partnership room—before and after! She and Mike had noticed some easing in the tension between them. They were continuing with counseling and both had experienced some major breakthroughs. What she was most excited about in terms of their process was what had happened to the Partnership area of their home (see *Main Floor–Final Plan*).

She explained she and Mike had tackled the room that very next weekend. They went through stuff from each of their college years, wedding presents they didn't need, broken chairs, and old clothes. Ninety percent of the items taking up space in the room were useless to them. They began throwing out and giving away until they were left with a small pile of treasures which had meaning for one or both of them. These things were easily incorporated into other parts of their house. To their surprise, they were able to accomplish this daunting task without one argument or even small bickering between them. And in the end they were left with an empty room!

They decided to incorporate the Feng Shui color appropriate to the Partnership area—pink. Since neither of them was wild about straight pink, they painted the room a dusty rose—a color they both loved and liked to wear. Mike's mother gave them an Oriental rug she no longer used which they put over the hardwood floor. They weren't in a position to buy a lot of furniture, so they had piles of pillows until something else came along. Mike, who was in the lighting business, brought home a discontinued line of sconces which he wired in four areas of the room. The lighting gave the room a soft, romantic glow. She was sure to tell me that they had hung a mirror to increase the Partnership area of the house. The more Julie shared the adventures of this room with me over the phone the more excited she became.

She and Mike used the room as a "Partner" room, she went on. They would go in there to talk, have a glass of wine, or process some part of their therapy together. Sometimes they would go in there to quietly think or read. The room had become a symbol of something more than just a cleaned out room. And it seemed to be having a positive impact on their marriage.

They had also moved their bedroom to the back of the house (see *Upper Floor–Final Plan*). They were both surprised at the difference it

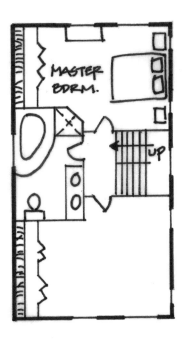

Upper Floor–Final Plan

made to their quality of sleep. It was hardly any inconvenience that the room was slightly smaller than the one they had been in. Before they moved their furniture into the back bedroom, they decided to paint the walls a deep taupe color to get away from abundance of the white walls in the rest of the house. Mike made a headboard and they found another nightstand. They removed all pictures of people other than themselves. They even framed and hung pictures of the two of them together which hadn't been displayed before. Those particular photos reminded them of particularly magical and loving moments in their lives together. Julie assured me that the bedroom was now her favorite room in the whole house. She had left it simple, a feeling she really liked.

Two-and-a-half years later, I am happy to report that they are still together. They courageously continued with counseling and working on their own issues for another year or so. They were both clear that their intention was to make theirs a solid and long-lasting marriage. I was deeply touched, recently, when I received an announcement of the birth of their baby girl.

Paul

Looking to the future

It was one of those dreary fall Friday
afternoons. I had immersed myself in a
blueprint that a client had sent me for consideration. By 3:00 PM I realized that everyone I knew must be hanging it up for the week as my
phone hadn't rung for a couple of hours. Around 4:00, when the
phone did ring, I expected it to be a friend or my husband. Instead, I
heard a male voice identifying himself as Paul. He had been reading
about Feng Shui and wanted some specific information as to what it is
and where it came from. I pulled myself out of my Friday lethargy
and began a conversation with an intense man who, despite it being
the end of the week, wanted to begin a new journey in his life.

Paul and I talked for nearly thirty minutes about Feng Shui in general and how it works. Finally, he asked if I'd ever consider doing an appointment in an efficiency apartment since that's where life found him right now. Contrary to the reaction of his friends and family, he was actually enjoying the experience and was in no hurry to move into a bigger place. We set up an appointment for a few weeks into the future.

Paul was actually a veterinarian who owned the building he was working in and had created a small apartment in the back of the space. Although a man in his mid-40s, he had just graduated from veterinary school with a huge debt load. This arrangement enabled him to live and work very inexpensively.

When I got there, Dr. Paul was just discharging a Golden Lab to its owner after the dog had undergone surgery. He took me back through his clinic, past a room of kennels of dogs in various stages of recuperation, an examining room, and a storage area. Suddenly, we were in his private space. It took me by surprise as there seemed to be no transition between work space and living space—a door opened and we were in.

His space was simply furnished, definitely small, and set up for extreme function. There were no frills. We sat at his kitchen table while he told me why he wanted a Feng Shui appointment. He had bought the building years ago and continued to have a retail business of some sort lease from him year after year. When he was ready to set up his veterinary business, he didn't renew the tenant's lease so he could claim it for himself.

He gutted the whole space to make an apartment for himself as well as re-configure the front area to suit his needs. With financial help from his cousin, he was able to get the space the way he wanted. He'd been working this way for a couple of years. The business was doing quite well. He had been able to hire an assistant after the first six months to help with the phones and customers. He wasn't interested in a relationship at this time in his life and money seemed to be going all right. So why was I here? Two months ago he was diagnosed with colon cancer. The medical consensus was that it was in early stages and with some aggressive treatment they felt they could arrest it. The dilemma was that Paul didn't want to treat his disease with traditional medicine but instead was using alternative methods to heal.

Despite his own medical background (or because of it), Paul was addressing this sobering fact with controversial means. He adopted a macrobiotic diet, was practicing qigong, using an acupuncturist, and having weekly hands-on healing sessions. Now he wanted to see if Feng Shui could address any issues which might be present in his space. Obviously his intention was to heal. Since the diagnosis had been rather recent, it was too soon to tell if any of his methods of treatment were making a change. He was convinced he was on the right path for himself.

Because Paul owned the building, I needed to not only look at his living space, but also the impact of the entire building to assess the total picture. We began in his living space first. He had been truly clever in his use of space—everything was in miniature size, yet workable. It was set up for a single person to live here efficiently.

When we isolated the layout of his apartment, it became obvious that Paul was living in a cleaver-shaped space—and sleeping on the knife edge of that cleaver. A knife edge implies cutting and slicing, a possible connection to surgery, just the treatment Paul was attempting to avoid. Because he owned the building, there were some aspects of his personal life which spilled over into the business. For instance, he paid all his bills and did any correspondence in the front of his office where there was a computer. He had no television in his apartment, but there was a small one in the conference/lunch room which he'd occasionally use to watch something special.

His living space was mainly for eating and sleeping. Due to his macrobiotic diet, Paul was concerned about the kitchen area and wanted to make sure there weren't any problems from my perspective. He had not been sleeping well lately but attributed this to his concerns about his health. The plumbing in the building was the one feature they

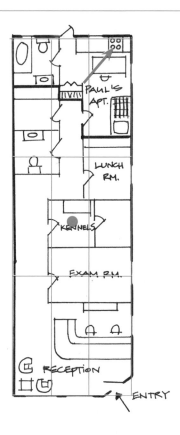

PAUL'S APT.

LUNCH RM.

KENNELS

EXAM RM.

RECEPTION

ENTRY

hadn't re-done during the massive remodeling. Sometimes the toilet made noises all night long which would keep him from getting a good night's sleep.

I suggested that Paul try to keep the kitchen counters as clean as possible. He had plenty of cupboard space available for a lot of the items which were scattered on the surfaces. By keeping these areas clean, he would be giving himself the continual message that the food he was preparing for his healing was wholesome and hygienic. I suggested a smaller table for the center of the area instead of the over-sized one he had crowded in there. I also suggested that, when at the table, he sit in a chair facing the entry door, so he would feel strong and secure at all times.

Paul also had a closet corner pointing toward the table and the food preparation area. This poison arrow could undermine any of his feelings of health and well-being as it has energy that is too strong in which to eat food. I suggested that he hang a crystal from the ceiling in front of the corner to provide a barricade for himself. I also suggested that he keep the bathroom door closed at all times. It was too close to the kitchen where food was being prepared and eaten. He didn't have any problem with that.

Since I didn't want him sleeping with his head on the knife edge, I suggested he move the futon to the other wall in the room. I strongly encouraged him to fold it up each morning to provide him not only more space, but also a sense of order. Because the space was small, I tried to impart to him the importance of keeping things in their place. Although he lived alone, it didn't excuse clothes hanging all over, an unmade bed, and things strewn across the counter. It was obvious that a second person would have a very difficult time finding room in this space.

I also suggested that Paul create some way to identify that he was entering his space from the clinic. Rather than walking through just another door, I suggested that he paint the door a different color from the others, or at least have a small brass sign that said "Private" engraved on it. He didn't see the point, but agreed to do so. I was trying to get him to balance his life between personal and public. As it was, business things were in his living area and personal things were in the office.

When we moved into the clinic, Paul lamented that he hadn't thought about things differently when he'd remodeled. He was in need of another veterinarian but had no room to incorporate anyone. In order for him to expand, he would have to sell the building and move. He presently found himself working 70–80 hours a week and didn't know how he would manage if his cancer became an issue.

I commended him on the rounded edge of the countertop as it prevented a poison arrow from shooting into the small waiting area he had in the front of the office. I also assured him that having a slanted door in a business was very good luck and that I wasn't surprised he was so busy. We located the center of the building which is where Health is reflected in the whole space. It was located in the kennel room. Unknowingly, Paul had positioned a wall running through the middle. On one side was the exam/operating room and on the other was storage and kennels. I suggested a painting be hung on the wall closest to the center, one that he was particularly inspired by and possibly one which had some yellow or gold tones in it, since that's the color representing the Health area.

The front area was a little chaotic. Some boxes of dog food had been delivered and not put away. Paul confessed that they'd been sitting there for two weeks. One of the chair seats had been torn by a frantic puppy being brought in for an exam. I suggested that it be repaired and that the front door be adjusted so it would be easier to open. I had to push against it with my back when I had arrived for my appointment. If I'd had a squirmy dog in my arms, I might not have enjoyed that experience.

We sat in front for a while talking about his business. He shared his views about his business, his personal life, and his cancer. It seems his father, an uncle, and his grandfather had all died at age 51. Paul was 49. The cancer seemed to have arrived right on time. Although all these other men died from different causes, Paul couldn't help but see a pattern. Suddenly something began to fall into place for me. I had been unable to put words to some kind of feeling I was having, but here it was. Paul had been preparing for his departure for several years. I told him so, but he didn't get where I was going.

Here was a man, two years away from what he suspected would be his inevitable outcome, working in a space where there was no room to move into the future with another vet, and living in a space where there was no room for a future relationship. He had set up the "dead end" all along. Unknowingly, of course. He looked at me as though I was crazy. "You need to make room for a future," I said. "I don't have room," he quickly threw back at me. "You'll need to find another place to live, use that space for another veterinarian, and move forward." I can't remember being that direct with a client before, but I could see no other way out for him.

I suggested that he still do the things we had discussed, but I strongly encouraged him to consider the possibility of moving. I left him with lots to ponder and hoped he would keep me posted.

Paul did keep me involved through his whole process: I helped in his selection of another apartment, setting up this new place with Feng

Shui principles in mind, and the remodeling of the clinic to accommodate another person. I even ran a Chinese horoscope for Paul and the new vet he was thinking of bringing in to check for their compatibility.

Paul did agree to some traditional medical treatments when he felt his health was beginning to falter. But for the most part he managed his own health care. He continues to do well and is very optimistic for the future. He loves his work now that he's not overwhelmed by it. He began dating a woman he knew from his college years who has been a great support to him during some difficult moments. He is now 52 years old—having crossed a huge landmark for him. His cancer is in remission and he is planning for next year—and the next.

Phil and Louise

Working at home can work

Phil and Louise had recently moved into a
newly constructed home. It was their first
home together as a married couple and they were excited about their
new life. Both Phil and Louise were self-employed, each operating
from a home office. Louise was a freelance writer and editor. Phil ran
a mail-order catalog business on the Web, selling computer parts.
Both enjoyed their work—until they moved in, that is.

After buying the house and getting settled, Phil experienced immediate frustration with his job. Despite various arrangements of his
office furniture, he could not find a comfortable place in which to

settle. He didn't even like being in the space and would find excuses not to go into his office. A hard and diligent worker, Phil was not one to blow off business. Understandably, it was beginning to affect them financially.

Their home was near the end of a little street in the development. Each day, sometimes many times during the day, they would drive by a sign which says "Dead End." This can become disheartening after a while. It doesn't take long to imagine you really are at the end of the road and can go no further.

Furthermore, their home was situated with the garage sticking out in front, hiding the front door. I did not actually see the door until I had gotten out of my car and walked around the garage. A basic principle of Feng Shui is the front door should be prominent and obvious. Not being able to readily and obviously see the door where opportunities and good luck flow into the space allows these fortunate events to pass by. Both this hidden door as well as the dead-end message may well be contributing to Phil's decline in business.

I suggested a wind chime be placed at the corner of the garage with a dual purpose in mind. First, it would keep things flowing in their lives and would negate the stagnation which can come from living on a dead-end street. Second, the wind chime would draw attention to where the door was located. I also suggested they move their address numbers from above the garage (where obviously they don't live) to the side of the garage closest to the front door. This would indicate the direction a visitor would take to get to the door. Also, it wouldn't hurt to place pots of flowers, shrubs, or lighting by the walk to attract the flow around the corner and up to the door.

Had I been involved in the actual siting of the house, I would have strongly urged that the house be built as a mirror image of what it was. That way the front door would be visible as someone approached, bringing the potential for more good luck.

When superimposing the bagua over the main floor, the garage also impacted the results by requiring the bagua to extend out to the front of the garage. This meant there were missing pieces in the Career, Family, and Health areas, and the entire Knowledge area was challenged. I suggested a mirror in the entry to "push out" the wall (see *Main Floor Plan*).

On the main floor of their home, Louise had set up her office in one of the spare rooms. She had painted it a soft lavender color, added lots of plants as well as a fountain. They had splurged on some new office furniture for her as well. It was obvious she loved this space. Unlike Phil, Louise was busier than ever with her business. In addition to this room, Louise was also setting up another room on this floor as a sewing and craft room.

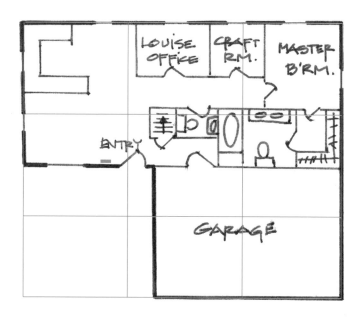

Main Floor Plan

Phil's office was on the lower level (see *Lower Level Plan*). When we went downstairs, they explained they hadn't been able to afford to purchase furniture for this additional family area but they hoped to in the next few years. Outside Phil's office was another large empty area intended to be their workout room when they could afford to buy the equipment. Phil's office was a small white room, with one little window. He opted not to buy any new office furniture, outfitting his area with a hodge-podge assortment of desks, tables, and file cabinets. He had his desk in one corner of the room facing the little window which set him up with his back to the door. I could see why he was uncomfortable in here.

We first discussed the furniture layout in his office. I explained the importance of being in a position to see the entrance. It signifies a sense of control in his life; he would not be caught off guard. I suggested moving the desk to the other side of the room and turning it around so he could see the entrance yet not be in the entrance. Phil stood in the middle of the room, trying to visualize this arrangement. He seemed frustrated trying to figure out a new layout. I heard him say under his breath something about being "pissed off." That clue sent me out the door to the room adjacent to Phil's office. A bathroom! The toilet was backed up to the same wall as his desk. Here was another reason to move his desk away from the wall.

Still, having discussed his furniture arrangement, I couldn't help but notice how desolate and forlorn Phil's "journey" was whenever he came down the steps to go to work. Despite their future plans, he was in an isolated and unfriendly environment. Louise's office was directly over him, adding to his oppression.

As I pointed out these observations, Phil became more and more agitated. At this point, he wasn't sure shoving around his rickety pieces of furniture would make him feel better. We discussed a possibility of

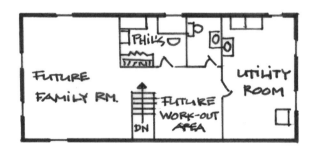

Lower Level Plan

setting him up in one of the areas they hadn't claimed yet (like the future family room or the future workout area) to give him more space. It would take considerable thought as to how to make it work and how to define the area, however. It was obvious to me Phil and Louise were going to have to talk through some issues in private. Phil was pacing back and forth by now, having looked at the reality of his situation.

The next day he called me to say they were considering putting the house on the market. It sounded like a drastic, knee-jerk reaction, but Phil finally was able to admit he'd never liked the place. Louise had fallen in love with it from the minute they saw it—and he got swept along in her excitement. All the things we discussed the day before brought to light his disappointment and anger with himself for having compromised so greatly. He was beginning to build up resentments against Louise and hadn't known why. He called to express gratitude for the enlightenment. At this moment, he wasn't sure there was a solution for him that would work in that house. He and Louise were considering their options.

Four months later, Louise called to set up another appointment. They were still in the house. A solution had found it's way to them in a most unexpected route. Phil's mother had died suddenly, leaving his father sad and distraught in the house he and his wife had lived in for over 30 years. After several family discussions, Phil's father offered to build out the lower level of their home as an apartment for himself. Meanwhile, Louise had noticed she hardly ever used the sewing/craft room. Her interests in that area seemed to have waned more than she realized. These two circumstances gave Phil the option to move his office upstairs. Louise wanted me to take a look at how Phil was setting up his office and she wanted me to look at the plans for the apartment.

Phil had already begun working out of the office on the main floor. I didn't need to ask him how things were going business-wise—I could tell by his face. And I could tell by his office. He had intentionally set up his space with new office furniture. He explained the furniture wasn't actually brand new. His father had given Phil all his beautiful furniture since he would be moving out of the house and wouldn't need it anymore.

Phil and Louise had had some heart-to-heart conversations after my initial visit with them. She was devastated to think about leaving her dream house. Initially, it seemed they had both been so excited. But as time went on, it became evident to both of them that Louise began to have the upper hand in their relationship. She took over many of the decisions they would normally have made together. She took over most of the financial responsibilities as Phil's business declined. She took over the upper floor as well. Moving Phil upstairs put them on a more equal status in more ways than one.

Louise was agreeable to having Phil's father live in their lower level. She got along well with him and was looking forward to getting to know him better. He, too, was a writer, so she felt they had a lot in common. Because her father-in-law was in good health and self-sufficient, she wasn't concerned about him making demands on them. Besides, for six months of the year he lived in his condominium in a warmer climate. With this new apartment he was putting in for them, he was not only increasing the value of their home, but Phil and Louise were also increasing the depth of their marriage.

Alice's Restaurant

De-cluttering an office and more

Seeing her youngest child graduate from high school, inheriting some money from her family, and selling the oversized house that had seen her through a 20-year marriage and divorce, Alice turned to the one passion she'd had all her life—cooking. It had always been a dream of hers to own a small restaurant, serving all-natural organic food. She took some of her money and leased a well-positioned storefront to provide the community with some of her outstanding culinary creations.

Alice maintained her belief in the integrity of natural and organic foods. Her cozy little restaurant was an immediate success. People came from across town to taste her homemade soups and fresh-baked bread. Her smiling face at the counter, along with her friendly banter with customers, brought even more people to the door.

One of her long-standing customers asked her to cater a major charity ball. Thus was born a secondary direction to her restaurant. Catering began to take more and more of her time. It also became the more lucrative side of her business. Her days would often be 16–18 hours long if she had to cater an event in the evening. Many mornings would find her in her kitchen at 4 AM baking bread. She had some part-time help, but they didn't have the passion she did. Alice was often single-handedly preparing lunches and dinners for the clients who came to her restaurant, while, in between, getting food prepared for a catered event for 75 people that evening. She had to admit, though, she was in her element.

But time was beginning to take its toll. Passion or not, a person can only keep a schedule of this intensity for a limited amount of time. Her typical orderly life was out of control. Her office was hopeless. She had no time to enjoy her financial success. For obvious reasons, she had to give her dog to one of her daughters since she was never home to care for him. It was after this heart-breaking decision that Alice called me.

We had to meet on a Monday because the restaurant was closed on Mondays. Alice basically wanted control and balance in her life again. She still loved every aspect of her business, but it had far surpassed her expectations and she couldn't keep up. Her office mirrored this situation.

It seemed most beneficial that we work in Alice's office since it reflected her energy more intimately than the restaurant itself. Her desk had stacks and piles of papers, mail, and canceled checks along with her computer. The floor was likewise filled with stacks of magazines, more papers, tax forms, etc., etc. A credenza was buried with boxes of sample dinnerware and cutlery which she had received. All of this stuff spilled over onto a small round table. It was hard to know where to begin.

Because Alice spent the majority of her time at her desk, I suggested that we start there. In an area overrun with clutter, I will usually tell a client about a Feng Shui method for clearing a space which involves removing nine items a day for nine days. The number nine is an auspicious number representing success and completion. Although it doesn't seem like much of an effort on a day-by-day basis, at the end of nine days, 81 things would have been moved, filed, tossed. The reason for doing a little each day is to build the momentum gradually. Alice was ready to move all 81 things that day and be done with it. Instead, by doing some action around this issue each day, she would reinforce a new pattern for herself. A habit takes a period of repetition before it sticks.

Before

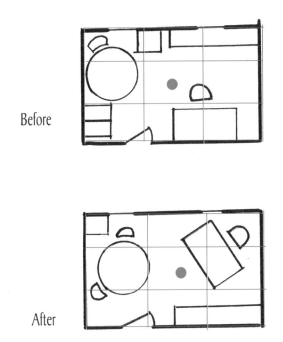

After

De-cluttering an office and more

I also suggested that she hang a crystal in the middle of her office (●) to balance and gently move the energy. She could also hang it with the intention of getting guidance and clarity to bring in the appropriate help she needed in her business.

Additionally, I suggested a new office layout she could implement at some point. As it was now, her desk was too close to the entrance. Alice had assumed a "gatekeeper" or receptionist position which left her susceptible to too much activity. Being so close to the door, a lot of issues could easily land on her desk. My suggestion was to move the desk to the back corner to alleviate this tendency. We agreed that a lot had to clear out before such a move could realistically take place.

Six weeks after my visit, I drove by Alice's restaurant and noticed a "Soon To Be Closing" sign in the window. I called her at my earliest opportunity. She sounded upbeat and spirited. She'd been meaning to call me but with everything going on she hadn't had time. I expressed my regret at losing a wonderful eating establishment in the neighborhood. Alice said that as she was doing her "nine items a day for nine days" process, she began to listen to her feelings and to her heart. After the first cycle of this clearing clutter method, she began a second round, when one day she just knew what she had to do. By the time she got around to moving her office furniture, her plan was ready. Although she loved the restaurant business and enjoyed chatting with and meeting new people, Alice saw how draining it had become to own both a restaurant and catering business. For the amount of effort and time the restaurant required, financially the returns were small.

Her catering business, however, still enabled her to meet people while she could continue to prepare culinary presentations. From a financial standpoint, the catering side of her business would provide her with a comfortable income without all the stress. The decision to close her restaurant was obvious. She would not have the torturous schedule. She would not have the overhead the restaurant required. She would need less hired help. And, more importantly, she would have more time to devote to herself and her family. She could even bring her dog back into her life.

As with many people, Alice's life got out of control before she recognized it was happening. By one standard of measure, she was successful and could be happy with the results. But by her own personal standards, things were not right. Shifting items in a cluttered and crowded environment can loosen up many things besides furniture and paper. It can also give room for clarity and new possibilities.

Wayne

Picking up the pieces

Wayne called me after hearing me speak at a local event. He had never heard of Feng Shui until the evening a friend dragged him to hear my talk. He was smitten by the concepts of Feng Shui and wanted me to come to his townhouse as soon as possible.

I didn't know what his feverish excitement was about until I got to his place. Five years earlier, Wayne and his wife had bought this townhouse as their dream home. A year ago, his wife died. He had come to terms with her death as she struggled with cancer for two years. At this point in his life Wayne was trying to figure out how to move on.

Wayne's townhouse was built so the garage protruded out in front, partially blocking the view of his front door. The master bedroom was situated over the garage on the second floor. He also had a multi-level layout in which the living room and kitchen were on one level, but the bedrooms were on another side-by-side level. Furthermore, when you entered through the front door, you were met by a split entry. Red flags were going off all around me.

Having a master bedroom in front of the front door sets up a pattern of separation between a couple. This separation might be the result of divorce or travel, maybe illness where one of the partners is in the hospital a lot—or death. A couple must struggle to stay together when they're sleeping so far forward in the space.

Added to that is the fact that they were sleeping over a garage. This situation does not give a couple enough support to maintain a solid relationship. There can be feelings of betrayal or abandonment between the two people. It doesn't feel safe to sleep over this large unsupported space. If one of the partners has a tendency or potential for illness (physical, mental, or emotional), sleeping above a garage provides a stimulus for bringing the weakness into reality, as it did for Wayne's wife.

Furthermore, a split entrance with its up-and-down staircase positioned by the front door is another pronouncement of health challenges.

Picking up the pieces

Wayne was surprised when I asked if his wife had died of breast or lung cancer. It seems it started in the lungs but metastasized to the breast. A split entry often hits in the chest area of a person's body. Despite Wayne's argument that she never used the front door, always entering from the garage, the pattern for this kind of health challenge was still present.

Another staircase in the center of the townhouse reinforced the instability of general health. And the position of the bed, with their feet pointing out the bedroom door and down the hall, contributed to health challenges. The *feet out the door* or *feet first* situation can imply death. The Chinese remove a person who has died in the home feet first to help them get on the right path in their next journey. This is not auspicious for people who are living.

Wayne assured me of two things: his own health was fine and he would like to stay in the space. He might want to re-marry someday. He had just begun dating again. Yet his late wife's presence was felt everywhere. Her picture appeared in every room. She had collected antiques, so the house was full of her treasures. Wayne hadn't moved or gotten rid of anything since her death.

Wayne listened to all I had to say. I assured him we could treat each of these situations with an adjustment so the energy would shift. A round, faceted crystal in the center of the townhouse would stabilize

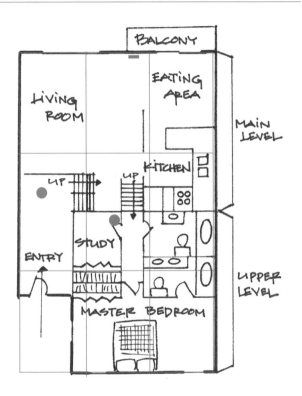

BALCONY

LIVING ROOM

EATING AREA

MAIN LEVEL

KITCHEN

UP

UP

ENTRY

STUDY

UPPER LEVEL

MASTER BEDROOM

the whole health area (●). Round shapes bring balance and harmony where there is unevenness. In fact, I suggested this as a priority activity. He could also hang another round, faceted crystal from the light fixture in the front entry to diminish the effects of the split stairs (●). We found a place to hang a mirror to energetically move the bedroom to the back of the house so it would not be as vulnerable to the street. I was suggesting a re-positioning of the bed, when Wayne said, "Maybe it'd be easier if I moved. I've been thinking about it. It might be the only way I can move on."

I could feel the wrenching courage it took for him to come to this conclusion. He understood that the townhouse didn't cause his wife's cancer. It simply provided numerous ways for it to grow. The fact that he was healthy was proof that not everyone would get sick and die in this place. But to have to adjust with so much intention seemed like it was more effort than he wanted to invest. Furthermore, he admitted that as long as he lived here he would never be able to begin another relationship.

I discussed some "when you are ready" suggestions with Wayne. When he's ready, he should replace the bed—mattress, box spring, sheets, pillows, all of it. Changing the energy in and around the bed lets go of a past intimacy to allow a new one in. When he's ready, he could make a decision about all of her antiques. He admitted that two of her sisters had asked about a few of the pieces. And finally, when he's ready, he could begin to put some of her pictures away. He needed to do these releases in his own time, I assured him.

Wayne did move. It wasn't long after our appointment that he put his townhouse up for sale. I saw him at another of my lectures. He was going to be closing on a new place within a couple of weeks so he came to pick up any new suggestions for himself. He looked at peace, maybe relieved, maybe a little sad. Wayne shared that he was keeping one antique chair he and his wife had bought together. The rest of the antiques he had sold or given away. A whole new bedroom set was being delivered to his new place the day he moved in. He still missed her and their life together, but it was time to move on. After my lecture, I felt sad watching him leave the room. By the time I had packed up my projectors and books to head home, I had gotten into a melancholy state myself, having thought about life's unfairness, tough decisions, and Wayne. I was just reaching my car in the parking lot when I saw Wayne chatting with two women from the lecture. He was expounding eloquently about the predicaments of his townhouse and his reasons for moving. The two women were obviously impressed with his insights. They had just decided to stroll over to a nearby coffee shop to continue their conversation when Wayne caught my eye. He smiled and waved. It was good to see that perhaps he was indeed moving on.

Jeanette and Will

Deserving abundance: What's in the garage?

Jeanette emailed me to get information about setting up an appointment. By the time I arrived at her house, we had communicated several times via the internet, without any personal contact. Her husband, Will, was also present at the appointment. It was obvious he had some concerns and doubts about the expense of doing a Feng Shui appointment, particularly when their reason for calling me was money challenges.

Will's job of twenty years had been downsized. He was given another position in the company, but at a lot less pay. He agreed to take the job until he could figure out another alternative. Jeanette was a real estate agent but for some reason, in the past six months when they needed the money the most, her sales had hit rock bottom. Because they were not making ends meet, they had been borrowing from credit cards.

Will and Jeanette had bought their house five years ago under ideal circumstances due to Jeanette's connections in real estate. They had purchased it from a bank as foreclosed property. The first owners relinquished ownership due to their own severe financial difficulties. Will and Jeanette were concerned about any lingering energy from their predecessors.

They had an attached double car garage on the side of the house that reflected the energy of Knowledge, Family, and Wealth (see *First Floor Plan*). One of the stalls was so full of belongings that both of their cars didn't fit in the garage. As I commented on the condition of this space and the importance of keeping it in order, Will explained that there were some boxes, like about six or seven, that had never been opened since they'd moved in. Jeanette took vigorous issue with that comment, assuring me that they had, too, been opened. There were simply things in there they didn't need right now. She couldn't

Deserving abundance: What's in the garage?

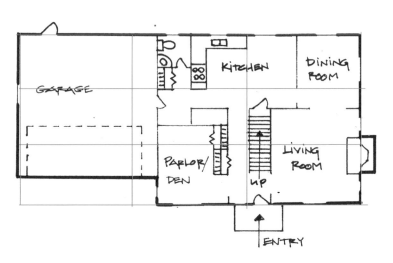

First Floor Plan

remember what those items were, but she was sure they might need them some time.

I tried to assure her that what was in the boxes wasn't the problem. The problem was their lack of usefulness to them. It signified a stagnant, dead area—just the kind of energy they didn't need in the Wealth part of their space. Storage was fine as long as they knew what they were storing and as long as it was something they wanted in their lives. If storage was the option they chose, then the boxes should be labeled.

It wasn't just those boxes that were the problem either. I began to ask about their plan for the miscellaneous furniture, bikes, and recycling. Well, they didn't have a plan. Jeanette's son had his own apartment and she was hopeful he might want some of the furniture, but so far he hadn't expressed any interest. Until then, this seemed as good a place as any to store these things. Of course, last winter it was more than a little annoying when one car had to sit outside all the time, despite the fact that they have a double car garage.

I strongly urged that they begin in the garage. Clean it out, sweep, and organize. I went so far as to suggest painting the garage floor to facilitate sweeping it out. Due to their financial state, Will and Jeanette were willing to try anything.

I also noticed that behind the piles and boxes there was a door leading from the garage out to the back yard. "Never use it," they both chimed. That being an irrelevant fact, I explained that having a back door in the Wealth area allowed money to get away, whether the door was used or not. Besides, once they'd cleared the stuff out of the way, they might find themselves going in and out of that door. For a back door in Wealth, a recommended adjustment is to hang a wind chime by the door, either inside or outside. A wind chime "calls" the money back into their lives. We walked around the garage to see what was going on in the back yard. A beautiful little maple tree was growing about twelve feet from the garage. One of its branches reached out toward the garage and the door in question. Jeanette decided a wind chime could be hung on that branch to resolve the money issue. She stood and looked around the area as though she were seeing it for the first time. "Why don't we put a little bench out here, maybe the birdbath that we've got stored somewhere in the garage?" I encouraged any attempts at improving the space.

Another Wealth challenge in Will and Jeanette's home was a staircase that came from the second floor and landed right in front of the front door. This feature presents another escape route for money—it is propelled out the door at great speed. I suggested that a round, faceted crystal be hung from the light fixture in the entry. The fixture was halfway between the door and the bottom step. A crystal would help to slow the Wealth energy from flying out the door. A round rug could also "detour" the flow of money. Or, because their entry was fairly good-sized, they could place an empty basket by the front door to catch all their money before it had a chance to leave. The basket needed to remain empty at all times and not become the repository for mail, keys, or mittens, I explained. If the basket became filled with items, there would be less room for money. Will and Jeanette opted for hanging the crystal.

It's not uncommon to see the same message transmitted repeatedly throughout a space. Thus far, Will and Jeanette had their Wealth area full of stuck energy in the garage. They had a back door leading money out of their lives, and there was a staircase by the front door. All of these features suggest a potential financial challenge for them. In addition, their predecessors had had a serious issue with money. We still had the kitchen and their bedroom to address.

There's a story in the Chinese tradition suggesting a connection between cooking and money: If a person were seen preparing a fire for cooking food, it was safe to assume that he must have had some money with which to get the food. If the person were preparing two, three, or even four fires, he must have had that much more money to buy so much food. In modern times, the burners on a stovetop represent the traditional fire and likewise hold the symbol for money. Only two of the four burners on Jeanette and Will's stove worked. They lost half of their money symbolically as well as in reality. The importance of getting the burners fixed was a low priority for them since they had been eating out almost every meal—until lately when budget constraints necessitated they eat at home more frequently. Will thought it might be something he could fix himself.

When we got to their bedroom (see *Second Floor Plan*), we all realized how uncanny this had become. Discovering the messages about money challenges that seemed so prevalent in their space Jeanette and Will could understand why their lives had taken such a drastic turn financially. In the back left corner of their bedroom, I noticed a large stain on the ceiling. A roof leak, which had been fixed on the outside, was still evident on the inside. Leaking water is equivalent to leaking money.

On top of that, the wastebasket had been placed in that corner, metaphorically throwing away any money they might have. Will would get right on repairing and painting the ceiling. Jeanette pounced on the wastebasket, moving it to another part of the room. When she moved the container, however, she noticed mold on the carpet. They surmised that the mold had started when water leaked down from the ceiling. The stagnant message around money once again made itself obvious.

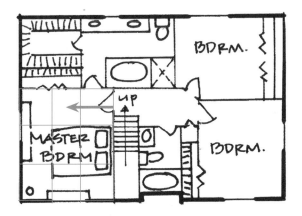

Second Floor Plan

Will and Jeanette were very clear about their intention around money. They wanted to return to the income they had before Will's change in jobs and before Jeanette's decrease in business. I suggested they buy nine Chinese coins since the number nine is a symbol of success and power. I instructed them to tie three of the coins together with a nine-inch red ribbon and place one set in the Wealth area of Jeanette's desk at work. Then I wanted them to tie three more coins together and place another set in the Wealth area of Will's desk. The remaining three coins would be placed singly under their welcome mat by their front door to set a theme of abundance and prosperity in their lives.

Because the money issues played out through their jobs, I also suggested a plant in their Career area to represent the growth they desired in their respective fields.

"Should we simply move?" they asked. "Wouldn't it be easier?" I discouraged their discussion around moving, for my concern was that they would take their issues with them. Instead, it felt important for them to stay and address whatever money challenges they were experiencing.

Jeanette and I had an opportunity to talk six months after our appointment. They had fixed the burners on the stove and had repaired the ceiling in their bedroom. They had hung a small, round crystal from the light in their entry. But it wasn't until they began clearing out a few things from the garage that Jeanette noticed an immediate shift in her real estate business. By the time the garage was done, she had surpassed her goals and was back on track. An interesting aside was that in clearing the old furniture out of the garage, she ran across her grandmother's china wrapped up in a box. Jeanette had forgotten it was there. Not wanting to keep it any longer, she had it appraised. The china was worth $5000. She eventually sold it to an antique dealer for $4950.

Will, however, struggled for quite some time in regard to his job. Whenever he had an interview set up, something would come up to prevent him from getting there. One day he was sick; one day the car overheated on the way to the interview, making him an hour-and-a-half late; and one day he just plain forgot. Meanwhile, Jeanette noticed how, after all their work, Will was starting to put things in the garage again. It seemed like self-sabotage was going on in regard to bringing money into his life.

Jeanette encouraged him to seek some counseling around this issue to see if that might help. Will discovered that, having grown up in a poor family, and watching his parents sacrifice and struggle, he had come to believe he didn't deserve an easier life. Rather than see an increased flow of money as an opportunity to help out his parents who were both living, he saw it as a discount to his upbringing. It was a hard, but real, revelation to Will which he continues to work on today. To assist him in this process, he works conscientiously to keep their garage in order. If his outer wealth message reflects order and flow, he can more easily take in the order and flow on the inner level as well. He can always tell if he's falling back into his old limited ways of thinking and feeling by the state of the garage.

Allison

Getting clear about a partnership

Allison and I were on the telephone for a few brief minutes to arrange for a consultation. Yet, during those few moments, she told me what she knew about Feng Shui, the history of her house, what she did for a living, and the reason she wanted an appointment. Her main goal was to find a marriage partner. I was to find out later that acting quickly and having high expectations were standard for Allison.

Four days before our appointment, Allison called me to say that she would be tied up on business out of town and wouldn't be getting back in time to meet with me. We re-scheduled for another time in a couple of weeks. Four days before that appointment, Allison called again to re-schedule. The third time she had to cancel due to business travel, I had to wonder how this woman would ever find time to nurture a relationship. I simply needed two hours of her time, whereas a serious relationship would require a lot more. From our brief conversations, however, I could tell Allison was a woman who knew what she wanted.

When I finally got to her place, she was most anxious to get me started on her relationship issues. Her house was a beautifully renovated lake cabin she had owned for three to four years. During that time Allison had gutted and remodeled the entire inside as well as redone the landscaping leading down to the lake. The remodeling was impeccably done with charming details that hinted at her financial investment. It was clear that Allison had spared no expense in getting the place the way she wanted it. In fact, she shared with me that she had hired and fired two contractors before the third one finally followed her instructions. The results were definitely worth it.

She and I walked through her main floor. I gave a few suggestions for some miscellaneous adjustments she could do to enhance the flow even more. Allison was furiously taking notes. A particular conversation occurred at this point that again triggered some doubts in my mind about her openness in fitting in a relationship into her busy life. I suggested she place a plant in her Wealth area to assure herself of continued abundance and prosperity. "No time to water a plant," she quipped, writing hastily all the while. She kept on moving down the hall. I didn't have a quick comeback, so I followed her to the next room. It was hard to argue with someone whose mind was so focused.

The Partnership area of the house happened to be in her bedroom. Like the rest of her house, this was a breathtaking room. I explained to Allison that having her bedroom in the Partnership area was very auspicious. I also explained that a traditional adjustment to call in a relationship was to hang a wind chime in the room. I assured her that, from the number of weddings I had attended, this adjustment has a good track record! The metaphor behind the wind chime was to "ring in" a partner, similar to a dinner bell chiming in people for dinner. Allison stopped writing and was looking at me. "You've got to be kidding," she said. "Who on earth ever heard of hanging a wind chime inside the house? They belong outside. That's why they're called WIND chimes. Get it? They need wind. How's that chime ever going to ring without wind?" I jumped in: "You could ring it." She looked me straight in the eyes for a moment. I thought she might actually be considering it. "Forget it" ended any hope of that happening.

I re-grouped. "The color associated with the Partnership area is pink," I began. "I hate pink." She cut me off mid-sentence. I re-grouped.

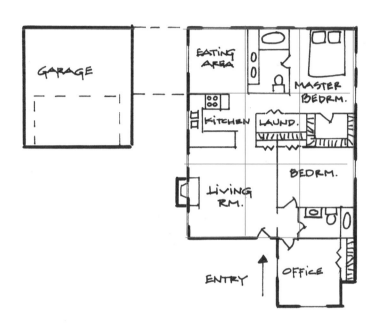

GARAGE

EATING AREA

KITCHEN

LAUND.

MASTER BEDRM.

LIVING RM.

BEDRM.

OFFICE

ENTRY

I pointed out that one of her bedroom windows was facing east. Hanging a round, faceted crystal in the window would catch sunlight, spreading rainbows of light and color all over her bedroom. It would be a symbol of the energy moving and changing. She had stopped writing again. I thought she might actually be liking this idea. "It sounds too New Age-y for me." I was going to suggest placing a plant in her room to symbolize growing a healthy and vital partnership. But based on her prior reaction to using a plant as an adjustment, I knew it wouldn't work.

I re-grouped in the only way I knew how. I turned to Allison and asked her what would symbolize a new relationship to her. Obviously, my suggestions were not succeeding. I reminded her that, whatever she chose, it needed to be something she loved to see. It could be big or small—bigger did not always mean better.

After giving this a moment's thought, Allison headed towards her china cabinet. She carefully removed a beautiful ceramic angel which measured about 8–9 inches high. She had bought it recently on a trip to Germany. The angel was equipped with a horn which Allison likened to a wind chime. Plus it was sporting a pink sash. I assured her that both elements were important and could support her partnership intentions. She was delighted. I was relieved.

The angel took its place on her nightstand with the intention of incorporating a partner into her life. I delicately reminded her how many times we had had to set an appointment before she was able to keep her commitment with me. I reminded her of her negative reactions to every suggestion I had made, indicative of a resistance to change. But she assured me that, if the right partner came along, she could and would make the appropriate changes in her life.

I took my leave of Allison, her impeccable little cabin, and her angel bravely standing in the Partnership area. Two weeks passed when I got a call from her. She was agitated and frustrated. She had come to the conclusion that the angel wasn't doing its job. She hadn't met a single prospect yet and was planning on taking the angel out of her bedroom. She wanted a partner and wanted him NOW. I strongly encouraged—insisted even—that she leave the angel in place. I talked to her about timing and allowing events to unfold in their right order. It wasn't what Allison wanted to hear, but she promised to let the angel do its job. "Patience is not my strong suit," she said. Oh really.

Six months passed before I saw Allison again. We ran into one another at a social event. Naturally, I was curious as to what had happened to her. Allison was quick to tell her story. It seems she met a man shortly after our last phone conversation, when she was questioning the purpose of the angel. She met him on one of her business trips, enjoyed his company, and spent some memorable times with him. A few weeks later, she met another man on a different business trip, enjoyed his company, had some memorable times with him as well. Life got complicated when she met a third man, this time in her hometown. She enjoyed him as well.

In typical Allison fashion, she juggled these three men for several months to see if there was one who ended up appealing to her the most. She managed to keep these men secret from one another, but it took a lot of effort on her part. She would see one for breakfast in one city, fly to another destination and meet someone else for dinner. They would call at different times throughout the week. She had to be conscious of remembering who she was talking to so she wouldn't call someone by the wrong name. She was hoping one of the men would be an obvious choice for her. They all began to demand more and more of her time and energy, until one day she had to make a decision.

Allison came to a realization and a remembrance from past affiliations of how much time, energy, and effort it took to be in a relationship. Even if she were just seeing one of these three prospective partners, it would require more than she was willing to give right now. Although she enjoyed their company, it was becoming obvious that none of these men was the right one for her. She broke it off with all three men and resumed her life as a single woman. She admitted to me how much she really liked her life and her freedom but hadn't realized it. In fact, she became so convinced of her decision that she returned the angel to its place in the cabinet. She was enjoying the peace and quiet, and some time to herself which she had badly missed.

As she was telling her story, I was thinking to myself how beautifully and gently Feng Shui can move a person to perfect clarity. Although it had seemed perfectly clear to me that Allison wasn't open to a partner, she went through her own process to discover it for herself. She seemed more relaxed and centered than she had during our prior conversations.

Should I by chance relish in this place of gratitude too long, Allison brought me back to earth. She smiled, patted my arm and said, "Too bad this Feng Shui of yours didn't work. Oh well, you tried." She turned and hurried off.

Anne

Moving on after a loss

Ever since she moved into her home four years ago, Anne explained, tragedy has seemed to be her constant companion. Within six months, her husband Frank had been killed in a car accident, her son Nelson was close to flunking out of high school, and her job had been down-sized. Although she had a job, it wasn't paying her adequately and she might be forced to look for another one. Money was a serious concern to her as Frank had not been foresighted enough to invest in any substantial life insurance coverage on himself. In addition, due to stress and/or the house, Anne had noticed a considerable decrease in her health.

She loved the house, but was seriously considering a move to another home. Anne blatantly asked if I thought the house was possessed.

Anne and Frank had bought this house as a model. Yet there wasn't much they would have changed had they built it themselves. They had previously lived in a smaller home in another part of the city. They wanted more space as Frank was beginning to do a lot of work at home and they needed an office for him. They also wanted to move before Nelson got into high school. The timing seemed right on all counts.

Before even superimposing the bagua on the space, I noticed a few features which could be a problem. First, upon entering, the front entrance lined up directly with two huge glass windows in the back. This feature is a potential for lost opportunities, implying that energy can get into the space but has a direct route out before it has a chance to bless the owners and the home. The lost energy can affect health, money, relationship, career, plus other situations. Anne needed to find a way to slow down this ch'i highway—with a plant in front of the window, a screen by the entrance to block the view, a crystal in the window, or some other element that could do the same thing. Anne moved a wooden, hand-carved, seven-foot sculptural piece in front of the window. It allowed light to get in around it, but it definitely kept one's eye in the space before moving on out to the porch.

I asked about her use of the formal dining room. "Never" came quickly and certainly. Having a food room (kitchen or dining room) so close to the front door is a potential for health issues. Since she never used the room, it would be better for her to designate it as something else—a library, perhaps, or a piano room. Anne was delighted to hear the suggestion of a music room, since her parents were planning to give her a grand piano which had been in their family for years. She had been concerned about where she would put such a huge piece of furniture, not having thought of the dining room. She would now have a place to position it beautifully, plus eliminate the negative health messages she was getting every day.

Her son Nelson had been sleeping in the front bedroom, the entire room being in front of the front door. When someone has a bedroom in this configuration, the person occupying that room does not feel like they're part of the family. There's always a sense of being abandoned. No doubt these feelings were magnified when his father died so abruptly. There was no particular reason Nelson was in that room, so I suggested he take the middle bedroom, which also reflects the strongest energy for the oldest son in a family. Anne could make that front bedroom into a guest room or home office.

In the master bedroom, Anne and Frank had placed their bed with their heads up against the wall in common with the fireplace that is in the great room. This situation is another health-depleting factor: the fireplace "burns up" their energy. Additionally, putting the bed against the opposite wall, common to the walk-in closet, gave Anne a better perspective on life—she could easily see the entrance to her bedroom from both the house and the porch. And, most importantly, it got her away from the fire.

When I laid out the bagua on her house, a few more issues came to light. In the Wealth area, Anne has a lot of drains, possibilities for Wealth to escape—the two sinks, the whirlpool, the toilet, and the shower. I suggested that she get some purple or lavender in the bathroom to counteract the drainage. The walls were already pretty neutral in color, so accenting with a deep eggplant color seemed intriguing to Anne. I also recommended that she plug up the drains when not in use to keep money from getting away.

The fireplace in the breakfast room is not a problem. Adding fire to the Partnership area feeds its energy and supports a loving relationship. Anne confirmed that their marriage had actually improved once they had moved into this house. Unfortunately, circumstances did not let them continue in this growth for very long.

We walked out onto the porch in the back of the house. Although it has three sides and a roof, it doesn't qualify as part of the bagua. I asked her about screening in the open side which was something she

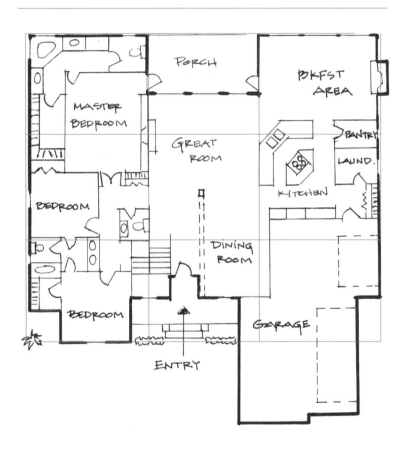

and Frank were going to do the first summer they were in the house. But when he died, she put that on hold. The Fame and Reputation area, which is located over this porch area, is considered challenged because so much of it is missing. The Fame and Reputation area is often connected to the Career area at the front of the house. Being down-sized or demoted in one's career, which had been Anne's experience, has connections to one's reputation. She decided to review the plan of closing in the porch. She had no doubt she would use it more when she screened it in, but she was even intrigued about making it a four-season porch for year-round use. I supported that idea wholeheartedly.

Speaking of Career, that area, too, was challenged due to the setback of the front door. I encouraged her to paint the door her favorite color. Anne really liked the idea of painting her door yellow. Besides communicating to the world her favorite color, it would also bring the door "forward" to fill up the missing area of Career. I also suggested that she landscape across the front to fill in the space.

In the kitchen, Anne's sink and stove were directly opposed to one another. This situation usually sets up some potential for arguing or disagreements. Living with a teenager, she nodded with a knowingness I could only imagine. I suggested that a round, faceted crystal be hung between the two appliances. Because a vaulted ceiling prevented this, we explored other options for easing the tension here. I suggested a round rug between the sink and stove. A rug that had all five colors of the Five Elements (white, black, green, red, and yellow) would also bring some balance.

The square column or pillar in the dining room was very close to the exact center of the Health area. It made good sense to find a way to enhance that square column. Being the creative person that she is, Anne decided to hand paint vines going around the column and onto the soffit that denoted the dining room space. She had done some hand painting herself in the breakfast room so this idea would fit with her theme. She agreed to add touches of yellow throughout the vines to stress the color for Health.

She has both an extension and a missing area in the Helpful People part of her house. The extension that sticks out in front of the bagua line is an extra blessing. The little corner set in on the side is a challenge. Anne has a missing area in the Knowledge corner as well. To "square off" the Knowledge corner, Anne was most open to landscaping outside in the yard, placing a shrub in the exact corner. She agreed to place a small mirror in the garage to "push" the wall forward and complete the missing Helpful People piece.

Because money was her most pressing need at the time, I prioritized the suggestions we had discussed so that dealing with the bathroom would be her first item. She was fine with plugging up the drains on the sinks and the bathtub each night. Keeping the lid down on the toilet didn't seem to be a problem. She also offered to get a round plastic drain stop for the shower. She was intrigued by the idea of bringing in some shade of purple or lavender in the bathroom to align with the color of Wealth. She was seeing purple candles, lavender towels and a rug. I could see she was getting the idea.

Anne invited me back three months after my initial visit. She had told me on the phone that she had been hired by a firm at nearly twice the salary she had been making doing exactly what she loves to do. The best part was that she got to work at home three days a week. She had transformed the front bedroom into her office.

When I arrived, I couldn't help but notice the lovely yellow front door. Anne had pretty well completed all the things we had discussed. But what she was really thrilled about was how she had transformed her bathroom. She couldn't wait to show me the purple/lavender theme. She was positive that all this intention in the bathroom was what brought about her job. The day she came home with her new rug and placed it on the floor of her bathroom to complete the picture, the phone rang. She was offered the job of her dreams! This extra money now made it possible for her to think about closing in the back porch.

Anne had also artfully painted graceful, winding vines on the center pillar of her Health area. Along with the painting, she had added silk vines to give a dimensional effect. The painted vines were extended into the music room where her grand piano was now sitting. The whole experience was inviting and warm. As so often with clients, I could see a new energy around Anne as well.

Her son Nelson took to his new bedroom very well. Things had eased between Nelson and Anne recently. He was spending a little more time with her and lending a hand when needed. Maybe he was just beginning to feel like part of the family again.

As we were concluding our time together, Anne asked the question I was expecting. I could tell she was somewhat reticent to bring it up. "Do you see any reason why Frank had to die? Could we have seen this coming and taken precautions? Could it have been the front door/back window line-up?" she asked. That alone would not have been an indication of something so tragic. "Could it have been our headboard against the fireplace wall?" Again, hardly a situation that would have caused me alarm. I assured her there was no one thing that contributed to his untimely death. It could have just been the drunk driver who hit Frank's car head-on, and took Anne's husband from her. Sometimes life holds mysteries we will never resolve. Feng Shui can change or shift some aspects of one's destiny, but there is always a bigger plan which unfolds no matter what.

The important thing was that she was finding her own life again and moving forward. One year after my second visit to Anne, she called me to say that she was re-marrying and was buying another house with her new husband, Riley. Anne's excitement was evident over the phone. Nelson would be graduating and going to college, so she wanted to begin anew in another house. She admitted to me that re-marrying had never been a goal of hers after Frank's death. But now that it was happening, she knew it was what Frank would want her to do.

Anne and Riley's story appears later in this book.

Ned

De-cluttering for a new life

When I first met Ned, he didn't know much about Feng Shui other than what he had read in a magazine. He thought it would be interesting to set up an appointment. Besides he was in quite a desperate state which required desperate measures.

On my way to his home, three things happened to give me a hint as to what lay ahead. First, a semi-truck had stalled in the middle of a city street a few blocks from my own house just as it was making a left-hand turn. Traffic was backed up for several blocks in both directions as cars slowly took turns getting around this obstacle. Second, when I finally got on the freeway, the ramp I was intending to take to

Ned's town was under construction, so I had to make a quick adjustment as to how I was going to get on the road I needed. Finally, despite what I thought were pretty clear directions to his house, I was unable to locate the address. As I drove around the area trying to get my bearings, I knew something unusual was going to happen on this appointment with Ned.

Unusual is not exactly the word I would end up using to describe the initial appointment. Everything looked fine, until the door opened. He was living in the upper part of a duplex, with tenants below him. It was apparent that the tenants were enjoying a loud rendition of some kind of rap music. The bass from their stereo made it seem like Ned's space had a pulse. He ran down the stairs to plead with them to turn the sound down. He told me later that he was embroiled in a severe battle trying to evict them.

As Ned ran downstairs, I had a chance to look around. It looked as though he had just moved in. There were boxes, bags, and piles of items stacked everywhere. There seemed to be nowhere to enjoy a meal as anything resembling a table was full of stuff. I found a small pathway to a bedroom where evidently Ned slept. I remained standing until he returned because there was simply no place to sit down.

Ned's story was pretty simple. Three to four years ago he divorced a woman for whom he clearly had feelings, moved away from the pain of it all, took a production job in this small town, bought a duplex and lost sight of his dreams. He was not well, obviously smoked, and was not very happy. He looked to me for some clue of where to begin to sort out his life. I tried to get him to talk about what he wanted, any goals he may have, where he saw himself in a year or two. But these questions were not within his realm of consideration. He only wanted immediate relief. The stalled semi, the closed ramp, and getting lost all began to make sense to me.

When in an overwhelming situation, the best plan of action is simplicity. I knew he couldn't take on some immense Feng Shui project. Besides I could sense that he was feeling a great deal of shame about the condition of his space now that I was standing in it. Yet, I had to believe he was ready for something to happen or else he wouldn't have called me. We had a brief introductory talk about what Feng Shui is, where it comes from, the importance of energy and intention. Ned tracked with me pretty closely. I suggested that we have a short initial appointment, let him implement a few small things and then I'd come back to consider his next step.

He seemed okay with this idea—relieved actually. The first thing I suggested was to hang a round, faceted crystal in the center of his space (see *Original Plan*). The intention behind the crystal was to calm and balance the space and to begin a gentle, subtle movement

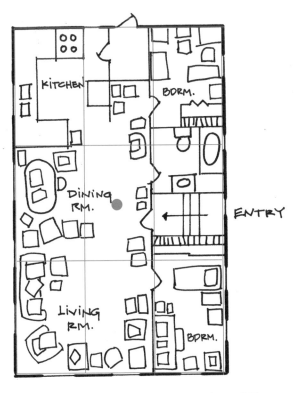

Original Plan

of the energy (●). Once the energy would start to shift, he would be more inclined to get unstuck himself and therefore deal with his clutter. We spent a few minutes measuring out his space to determine where the exact center was located. He said he would get the crystal the next time he was near a store.

That seemed simple enough. My next suggestion was to consider moving his bedroom. He currently was sleeping in the front of his house and was quick to tell me that he didn't sleep well—some nights not at all. I suggested that he take the room near the back of his space where it would be quieter and safer for him. It was a smaller room, but I was sure the advantages would outweigh the disadvantage of the size. He was starting to raise an objection to having to move all the stuff from one room to another, but I reminded him that all I wanted him to move was his bed and a dresser and leave everything else behind. The books, computer, treadmill, boxes of miscellaneous things, his gun collection and a television were NOT to be moved into his new room.

Of course, he needed to move out all the things he had in the back room. I suggested that he might want to clean the window in that room, shampoo the carpet, and maybe even paint the walls before moving his bed in, symbolic of a fresh start. He didn't seem too daunted by this switch; puzzled maybe, but not daunted. Besides all the stuff in the back room would blend nicely with all the other things stacked around!

That was all I wanted him to do for now. We re-scheduled another appointment for a month later.

Although open to the idea of energy and its potential impact on a person, Ned was relatively new to the concept of working with the environment. Feng Shui sounded like the solution to his problem of feeling overwhelmed, tired, and in need of a direction.

I returned to Ned's home a month after my initial visit. Ned immediately showed me the crystal he had hung in the center. He wasn't sure he had done it right and explained in great detail how hard it was to find a crystal and how long it took to find the right little nail from which to hang it. But he seemed quite proud of a job well done.

He was anxious to show me his new bedroom (see *Final Plan*). I couldn't help but notice on the way to the back of the house that not much of the clutter had changed and that the boxes and bags hadn't been moved. Nevertheless, Ned had managed to clear the back bedroom and had moved his bed into the back corner furthest from the door (the command position). He had indeed moved only one dresser in there as well. In cleaning the carpet, he realized that it wasn't tacked down very securely and underneath were beautiful, pristine hardwood floors. So the carpet was removed. The walls had a lovely coat of green paint and the window was sparkling clean. He showed me how it now easily opened up and down where before it had been stuck. Repairing anything broken or malfunctioning supports a smoother, less aggravating life. Ned seemed tentatively proud of his accomplishments, again not sure if he had done it right. Ned did admit he may be sleeping a little better in this room. Of course, he was quick to add that the tenants' stereo was no longer directly under his bedroom so naturally it would be quieter. I let it go at that.

I made a couple of additional suggestions for the bedroom—like bringing in a chair so he could sit by the window. I also recommended that he move his bed away from the wall so he could get in and out of bed on either side. Doing that brought the bed out into the room a little more than Ned thought was practical. He was willing to consider leaving it out in the room when I explained the importance of having options in life—even when getting in and out of bed.

The next area of concern was where Ned ate his meals. He made it clear that it was a stupid question since the kitchen table was buried with stuff as were the chairs. He ate on a recliner in the living room in front of the television. I explained that, whether he ate there much at all or not, he still needed to have a special place designated for eating food. He realized that meant cleaning off the kitchen table. I encouraged him to not just move the stuff to another part of the house, but to make some decisions about these things with regard to keeping them or not. He reluctantly agreed with me that it would be a good project, but I could tell it seemed monumental to him. I suggested he deal with nine items on the table—either move them, throw them, give them away, or file them. Doing this for nine days could make an incredible impact on his space. Nine items didn't seem so bad he assured me. Even the nine days didn't seem like too much to ask.

While still in the kitchen, I also relayed the story about the Chinese belief that if the burners on the stove are working and clean, he can expect more money and better health. Additionally, cooking good and nutritious food enabled a person to be healthy. Therefore, it is important for the stovetop burners to be in good working order. From the looks of the stove, I could assume that the possibility of having all four burners in working condition, even if they were scrubbed clean, was slim. Dealing with that stove was going to be a major project.

Along with the kitchen table and chairs, I could see Ned had had enough. I figured if I made too many suggestions as to what to change and what to move, he would fall back into the overwhelming state he was already experiencing in other parts of his life. Before I left, Ned was anxious to schedule another time for me to return. Was that a little enthusiasm behind his quiet demeanor?

De-cluttering for a new life

As I returned home, I recalled the obstacles I had encountered on my way to Ned's place the first time. Returning to the metro area, I drove by a field of wildflowers and remarked on their beauty—the first sign of spring and new beginnings. What a contrast to my first visit.

As I was driving to Ned's house for the third time, I couldn't help thinking how different this appointment was playing out from all of the others I do. Without words, he made it quite obvious that he needed to incorporate changes slowly, steadily, and in small steps. He also liked the fact that someone was monitoring his progress. I was anticipating the changes he might have made after our last visit together. I was curious as to what he did with his stove and his kitchen table.

Ned greeted me with anything but a pleased look on his face. I feared he might have gone into overload and become discouraged and disgusted with the whole process. He explained that his frustration was directed toward the stove which had become more of a project than either one of us had anticipated. In trying to fix one of the burners himself, Ned had disconnected the stove and pulled it out into the middle of the kitchen. He realized fixing it wasn't something he could do on his own. The stove had been sitting there for over a week while Ned waited for a repairman, making it impossible to get around in the kitchen.

Ned seemed disappointed that he hadn't accomplished everything we had talked about. We discussed the significance of getting to the bottom of a situation that hadn't been right since he had moved in. He knew he would feel good to get that part of his life in order.

As I turned around to check out what else he might have shifted in his space, I saw a spotless round table with four matching chairs placed neatly around it. He seemed quite satisfied with himself and found it funny that I was so surprised—shocked might be a better word. The huge table that had been piled full of clutter actually folded down to a round one once all the leaves were removed. Somewhere, he had unearthed a tablecloth (never mind the cigarette burn) and had graciously set out two bottles of spring water and a package of Oreos. I dare say I was probably his first "dinner" guest.

While enjoying the Oreos, Ned admitted quite sincerely that he had never slept as well as he now was in his new bedroom. He had placed a little plant by the window and enjoyed the element it added to the space.

It seemed peaceful in his place that afternoon, despite the still present stacks of things that were scattered around. When I commented on this, he told me that his noisy tenants had mysteriously agreed to move out without any further trouble. His new tenants were a couple who worked all day and were very quiet in the evening. He was understandably delighted at this change, and conjectured that maybe the crystal he hung in the center of his house might have created some kind of field that evicted the offensive tenant. He started to chuckle at the thought of that idea and then stopped, realizing it might actually be true.

Ned and I looked around at the rest of his space. His next concern was the front bedroom where he used to sleep. He had decided to make it into an office for himself, although his job at the manufacturing plant would probably never require him to have need for an office. He had already begun building bookshelves along one side of the room. He got excited about putting his computer in there with some books and a desk. We talked about the position of the desk and, like his bed, I suggested it be situated so that, when he was sitting at his desk, he would be able to see the entry door to the room. This would require that the desk be out in the middle of the room, which didn't seem like a practical idea to Ned. I also recommended that he curb some of his enthusiasm for building the bookshelves to the ceiling. By lowering the height of the shelves, he wouldn't feel so overwhelmed when he was in his office.

The bookcases would, in the end, be a significant tool for Ned. It would enable him to sort through his books and old magazines and make some decisions. Despite his excitement about having plenty of bookshelves, I suggested he build one less than he thought he would need. That way, he would be forced to consider more seriously which books to keep and which to release. He might think twice about keeping some books if it required that he build another shelf. Less is more.

Like the bedroom, we discovered that there were beautiful hardwood floors under a rag of a carpet. Ned had decided on a soft coral color for the walls and together we decided a small strip of track lighting would work for his needs. I could tell he wanted me to leave so he could get started on this room.

Although I wasn't sure why, I agreed to go back one final time within a few weeks. He was insistent that I'd want to see this beautiful new office when he was done. As I drove back home, I thought that maybe I'd cancel our appointment together since this was such a long drive, and instead chat with Ned on the phone to see how he was doing. After a week or so, I decided to keep our appointment. I had to admit I was anxious to see how his office was shaping up. Besides he might have some of those Oreos left.

This fourth and final visit with Ned was really just the beginning for my new friend. All he had needed was a starting point. Once he began to see and feel the difference in energy, he didn't need my input anymore. As I was driving to his house, I reflected how Ned proved to be a great teacher for me—about process, about productivity, and about patience (mine and his). I knew I couldn't keep

De-cluttering for a new life

driving out to see this dear man every few weeks for sooner or later he would need to assume his own power.

The last time I was there Ned was about to set up an office area for himself. I didn't have to wonder how things were going. When I drove up he was coming out the front door with a couple of bags to throw into a dumpster he had parked in front of his duplex. He looked pretty proud of himself as he waved at me. It seems the office project, although not quite complete, had lead to a major sorting and de-cluttering bonanza. Three bookshelves were done and in place with selected books placed neatly on them. As Ned found the energy to sort through his books and magazines, he realized he was going to need a dumpster to haul away all the old stuff.

In one of my earlier visits, I had casually suggested a Feng Shui adjustment in dealing with clutter: remove nine items a day for nine days. At the time, I wasn't sure that Ned had paid attention to the suggestion since he hadn't responded or written it down. But, contrary to what I thought, he had listened. Due to the amount of clutter, each "item" for him was a bag filled with useless stuff. Every day he had been taking out nine bags of stuck and stagnant energy, releasing some old and painful ties to the past. Six days (54 bags) had passed since he began this process. Ned was exuberant and almost unrecognizable!

He couldn't walk me into his house fast enough. His plans for the office were becoming elaborate, but not overdone. He showed me the repaired stove, the kitchen table still relatively uncluttered (placemats, too!), new blinds for his bedroom, new rug for his office. I couldn't believe the change in the place, evidenced in Ned's new energy. He actually had living room furniture which I hadn't been able to see before. We discussed some kind of storage system in his closets since clearly there were items he wanted to keep.

We spent about thirty minutes together moving some of his living room furniture to make it more inviting. All of the furniture had been pushed up against the walls, so I suggested pulling the couch away from the window and angling a chair on one side. He would eventually need some additional lighting and a coffee table. But for now, he had a place to sit and relax.

I left that day without another set appointment. I felt a little sad but had been reassured that he would invite me back in the near future. Ned called a few months after this last visit to say that, after he got his office all set up, he was promoted from production to sales at his company. He would need that office after all as he would be working from home.

We explored the idea of a new relationship for a moment. He decided that he needed to find himself, let go of the past, and create

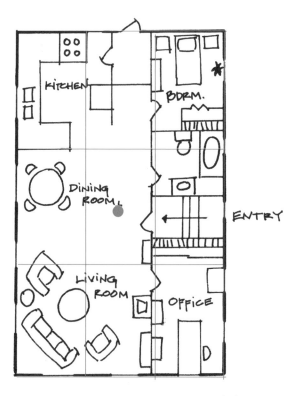

Final Plan

166

some of his own dreams before getting involved with anyone else's. It's now been over a year since our visits together. During a recent phone conversation, he told me he's still sleeping well, eats dinner at his kitchen table, and now enjoys the company of a cat. But the most profound event of all that happened to Ned occurred one morning when he woke up and habitually reached for his cigarettes. Since he was forced to get up in search of matches, he was struck by the beautiful space he had created as he walked out into the living room. It was orderly, uncluttered, and energetic. He looked around and realized that this was not the home of a smoker. That morning he quit smoking. If he ever felt any pangs to start again, he just needed to look around at his space. He had created a new message to himself—one that did not include this habitual activity. As Ned de-cluttered his house, he de-cluttered other baggage in his life, like smoking. This was an unexpected change for both of us, proving to me once again the basic Feng Shui principle that your space reflects your life.

One final note: right before writing this last phase in the life of Ned, I called him to see what was going on. He was dating someone and was madly in love. Go, Ned.

Evelyn

Claiming your space

Evelyn wanted a Feng Shui appointment because her house didn't feel right, even though she and her husband had lived there for seven years. Despite her husband's objections, she was having a consultation as a birthday gift to herself.

I began by asking her about the house history. Since they had only lived there for seven years, there could rightfully be some impact from predecessors. Evelyn corrected my assumption, explaining that, as a couple, she and Arnie had only lived in the house for seven years; but actually, Arnie had lived here for over twenty years. He and his first wife had built the house together. They had continued to live there for ten years or so until she died. Arnie had kept the house, living by himself, until he and Evelyn were married.

Evelyn had also been widowed five years ago and had been living in a small apartment. When it came time for them to make some future plans, it seemed practical for Evelyn to move into Arnie's house. It was bigger than her apartment, almost paid for, and easier than trying to buy another house.

Because Arnie had a full house of furniture, kitchen supplies, even linens, he figured Evelyn would be delighted to get rid of all of her things and simply move in with her clothes. She figured she should be delighted at this arrangement as well. So she moved in with only a few treasures of her own and her clothes. But now that she had been living here, she couldn't figure out what was wrong. She had been feeling exhausted, tired, even depressed. She couldn't imagine what was wrong.

We walked through the house together. Everything I asked about (a piano, a particular painting, an antique), Evelyn would share that it had been Arnie's or Arnie's wife's. Finally, I asked her to show me what exactly was hers. She took me to a small upholstered chair in the bedroom. The chair had been her mother's and Evelyn loved it. There were actually two chairs, but since there was only room for one, the other chair was in the basement. She also showed me a painting she had bought many years ago which she absolutely loved. It was in the guest bathroom.

I looked at this sweet woman and said, "Evelyn, you're living in another woman's house." Evelyn took that statement in quietly as tears welled up in her eyes. "You're a visitor in your own house," I continued. We sat down again to discuss her options.

She assured me that she and Arnie had recently discussed selling the house in order to buy some property together. Arnie, being practical and conscientious about their finances, convinced her that staying was the best option. He didn't know why she was unhappy— and she didn't exactly know either. But he felt strongly that it was in their best interest to stay in the house.

Evelyn began to share some of her story with me. Over the years she managed to change some things, but not without a struggle. After she moved in as Arnie's new wife, she insisted that all pictures of him and his first wife be removed. Arnie hadn't done it because his kids got upset whenever the pictures were gone. Clearly, they hadn't wanted their father to re-marry. Even after seven years, Evelyn still felt their resentment.

Evelyn had to clear out some of Arnie's first wife's clothes that were still hanging in her closet. Arnie had just "never gotten around to it." The bed they were sleeping in was the one Arnie had purchased and shared with his first wife. The paint choices throughout the house, the wallpaper, the carpet, were still all hers. "Do you like the choices she made?" I asked. "They're not my taste at all," Evelyn answered. Change is hard for Arnie, she explained. Any time they had a discussion about remodeling or repainting, he resisted the mere thought of it. His kids obviously supported his viewpoint.

There were boxes in the attic, boxes in the basement, and boxes in some of the closets as well. Evelyn would look in them sometimes, realize they were memories from Arnie's prior life and would close them back up again. She didn't feel it would be right to throw this stuff out so the boxes were left as they were.

Mail still came to the house addressed to Arnie and his first wife. He didn't see the importance of going to all the hassle of deleting her name from postal records. Evelyn wondered what else he owned that might still have his first wife's name on it—his life insurance policy, the house deed, his will. It wasn't hard for her to realize that her discomfort was being caused by her visitor status and by Arnie's seeming indifference to her feelings. She did assure me that she loved Arnie and was positive that, despite his behavior, Arnie also loved her.

Since we couldn't change Arnie, we could devise a plan for Evelyn. When I asked if she had a favorite room in the house, she assured me that there weren't many places she felt comfortable. But there was one small guest room she could be in. It had a lovely view of their back garden, was hardly ever used and, in her words, was the least obnoxious of all the other rooms. We went there to look at it a little more closely.

"A lot of guests?" I asked. Just one of Arnie's daughters who would come and live with them between jobs. This was her old room. I gently introduced the idea of Evelyn claiming the room for herself. I knew there were several other options for her stepdaughter, having seen the size of the house. The thought of it intrigued Evelyn. It was both exciting and frightening. It would necessitate taking a stand with not only Arnie but also with his daughter.

We discussed what could happen in this room. I first suggested that she remove the furniture to eliminate the feelings of it being a guest room. She could then repaint with her favorite color. The first two things I wanted to see in the space were her two favorite chairs and her painting. From there, she could decide what else might work. Evelyn didn't need to be told what she would do in the room. She was already envisioning herself reading, journaling, maybe praying. Just being alone in a space that supported her would be a big relief.

Evelyn's story slowly but steadily unfolded over the course of eighteen months. She tactfully presented the idea to Arnie, choosing just the right moment to discuss the specifics. He didn't understand but

agreed the furniture could be removed. More importantly, he agreed
to tell his daughter to adjust her expectations the next time she showed
up intending to move in. Evelyn went to work. The walls were painted
a beautiful blue, her favorite color. The carpet was torn up and
replaced. The two chairs were brought in as well as the painting. Over
time she added a small bookcase, a lamp, and some plants. Every once
in a while, Arnie would ask if he could join her in her special room.
She gladly brought him in. They would have tea and discuss the back
garden and other things—like his will and the deed to the house. After
a few months of this, Arnie stood up one day and said, "I don't know
what you've done in here but it sure feels good." He gave his okay
when she asked if she could also redo their bedroom.

At our first appointment, I had told Evelyn that their bedroom
would be the next priority after her own special room had been completed. She was free to move ahead now. After lots of discussions,
negotiations, tension and compromises, the bedroom set was given
away. She and Arnie purchased a new one together—one they both
liked. Per my suggestion, the bed had a solid headboard symbolizing
their support for one another.

The walls were repainted a golden yellow, new carpet, new bed
comforter, and pillows were purchased. Arnie was ecstatic about the
new look. Evelyn shared with me that at times she surprised herself

how she would hold firm to what she wanted. Her pattern had always been to give in to Arnie.

Eventually they remodeled their kitchen. Arnie loved the new look she was bringing into the house and couldn't wait for her to do another room, and then another, and on and on. Evelyn grew to love the house. All of her changes removed any trace of Arnie's first wife. The boxes were sorted and the contents distributed among Arnie's kids when appropriate. Much of Arnie's old life held in these boxes was no longer meaningful or memorable to him. Their relationship solidified. Evelyn felt complete support from him for the first time.

On their ninth wedding anniversary, Evelyn was shocked to hear Arnie toast his spunky wife. She had considered herself anything but spunky. Somewhere along the way she had found her own voice, however. And she felt good about it. Obviously, more than just the house had undergone some major changes.

Anne and Riley

Beginning again

Anne contacted me because she was
buying a home with her new husband.
Having remarried after the death of her first husband, Anne wanted
to start fresh in a new home, not one in which she had lived, and not
one in which her new husband was living. She called me to look at a
house they were considering.

I first met with Anne and Riley over a cup of coffee. They brought
their blueprints for me to look at since they hadn't been able to contact the current owners to allow us into the house. The current
owners were being transferred to Europe after having lived in the
house for ten months. The wife was torn about leaving since she

adored this home. Moving to Europe wasn't entirely unattractive, but she had invested a lot of energy in the house. The husband was thrilled to be making this move as it not only meant new adventures for them, but it was a substantial promotion for him.

Anne already had some ideas for changes. A feature she had come to love in her old house was an enclosed back porch (see *Main Floor Plan*). So, she wanted to enclose the deck, but wasn't sure of the impact on the house. She also wanted to designate an office for herself as her job still enabled her to work from home several days a week. They wanted a guest room and a library. They had enough bedrooms to do all this, but they weren't sure of the choice of rooms for the specific activities.

There were only a couple of similarities between Anne's old house and this one—the garage projecting out in the front of the right side of the house and a set back front door. But that was about the extent of similarities. The new house was a two-story with all the bedrooms upstairs. The kitchen was in the Wealth area.

I saw that in the center of this home, on the first floor, was a powder room as well as a staircase. The toilet landed almost exactly on the center point of the space. Both stairs and bathrooms are a challenge to the health of the family living there. We needed to address this issue first. I assumed neither feature would be moved considering

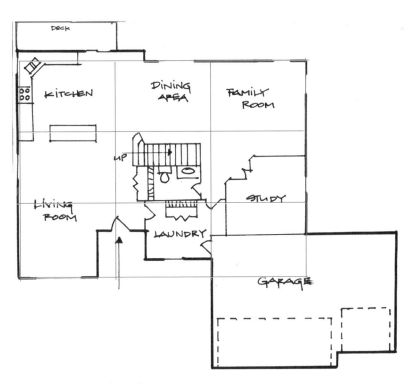

Main Floor Plan

the amount of effort it would take to do so. They assured me that moving the bathroom as well as the stairs had not been in their plans.

We first discussed the bathroom influence. A bathroom in the middle of a house can "drain" away the energy around health. Another metaphor I hear is feeling "flushed" of all energy or vitality. There are many possible counteractive actions that can be taken to offset this drain. First, I prepared Anne and Riley for trying to keep the bathroom door closed at all times. Her objection was that there was no window in there and that it might feel stuffy if the door was kept closed all the time. They were willing to consider it, however. Due to the seriousness of having a bathroom positioned in this area, I also suggested they hang a mirror on the outside of the bathroom door to bounce back any energy from getting in there and being flushed away. They'd think about that as well.

Anne remembered the bathroom being decorated in greens, a color she wasn't particularly fond of. Since the color for the center Health area is yellow, I offered the suggestion that she paint the bathroom yellow, or use yellow as an accent color. She resonated to that idea. I also suggested that she get her paint brush out again and re-create some of the beautiful vines I had seen her paint on the walls in her bathroom and her music room of her former house. I wanted these vines to be growing upwards to counteract the downward flushing action of the toilet and the sink drain. She didn't need any coaxing to put this idea together.

The staircase was also falling in the center of the Health area. This "up and down" situation could potentially become their health story. When an unevenness is occurring in a space, a round or oval object helps to balance the energy. I suggested that a round rug be placed at the foot of the staircase. Due to the hardwood floors in this house, a rug would be a beautiful addition. They wondered about a round rug at the top of the stairs as well. It wouldn't hurt, I assured them. In fact, a round rug at the top of the stairs would be the Health area of the second floor so it would be particularly helpful.

As far as room assignments on the second floor, I suggested that Anne's office be in the front bedroom *(Bedroom A)*. This room is partially over the garage, but since it was not being used as a bedroom, I didn't see that as a problem. Sleeping over a garage does not provide enough support for a person and can bring up issues of abandonment and feelings of separation. These feelings can all lead to ill health. But using a room over a garage where a person is awake and conscious does not impact them in this way.

I suggested that the next bedroom *(Bedroom B)* be a guest room and the remaining one *(Bedroom C)* be their library. Guest rooms are appropriately placed near the front end of the house so guests do not

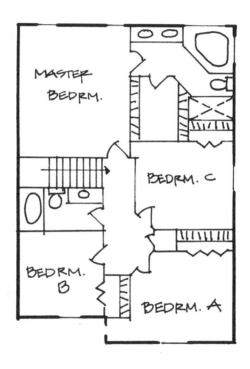

Second Floor Plan

feel overly welcome and then never leave. Both the energy of Anne's work and the energy of guests coming to visit should have some separation from Anne and Riley's personal space.

This was all we discussed about their new home on the initial visit. They were planning to finalize the purchase within the month. Meanwhile, Anne was having trouble selling her current home and asked about some suggestions. She hadn't begun packing yet, as she didn't want boxes sitting around when people came to look at the place. I encouraged her to let go of that perception and to begin packing anyway. People would see that she's on her way out and would understand that she's serious about moving.

I also recommended that she begin in the basement where so much of the past and old memories are often stored. And I suggested that any personal pictures of her and her family be carefully packed and put away. She needed to remove anything that had her name on it, such as a welcome sign or welcome mat. In other words, Anne needed to neutralize the space so other people could see themselves in it and not feel like they might be kicking someone out of their special home. This, of course, would bring up some painful passages of sorting through some of Frank's things (her first husband who was killed in a car crash). But, it would have to be done at some point. As soon as she was free of ties to the past, she would be free to sell the house. I wasn't suggesting she throw out the past, just deal with it and sort through it. I could tell Anne understood what I was talking about. Procrastinating wouldn't make it go away.

Since Anne and Riley were beginning a new relationship, I strongly urged that they buy a new bedroom set if financially possible. They had planned to use Riley's, which he had bought a few years ago while he was still married to someone else. I suggested that if they didn't buy an entirely new bedroom set, then at least buy a new mattress and box spring. If not that, then at least new sheets, pillows, and pillowcases. With this new realization, I could tell that Anne definitely did not want his old bedroom set in her new house.

The next time I met with Anne and Riley, it was in their new home. They had been living there for almost six months. Since our last meeting, they had gotten married, sold both of their own homes, and moved into this new one. They both looked radiant as they showed me around their house. One of the first things they did after moving in was to hire a contractor to build a screened porch over the deck. They also extended the deck to go behind the family room. I had assured them that by building the porch, they could extend their Wealth area dramatically. As a deck, without roof and sides, it doesn't impact the space in their house. But by enclosing it, the porch influenced the energy in the house, giving them the potential of earning or inviting in more money.

Anne was particularly pleased with the powder room. She had painted all the walls a soft yellow and, as I had hoped, she had put her artistic talents to work. Anne had hand painted delicate vines around the mirror over the sink and coming up from around the toilet. She had skillfully painted a few on the opposite wall to balance the effect. The vines had some brighter yellow flowers incorporated along with lavender ones. She had outdone herself and I could feel her pride. They also found a way to keep the door closed by simply putting scented candles in the room. Even unlit they provided a freshness to the room whenever anyone walked in. Riley had put a door knocker on the door so someone could knock before walking in. Otherwise, they felt it would be difficult to know if someone was using the bathroom or not since the door was kept closed all the time. They also had the word "Toilette" engraved in script lettering on the knocker in the place where someone's name would ordinarily be located.

A round rug had found a spot at the bottom of the staircase. Anne's office was nicely set up with the desk positioned in such a way that she could see the entrance to the room as well as see if anyone was coming up to her front door on the main level. They had not bought a new bedroom set. Instead, Anne and Riley had together painted the one he had. They painted all the furniture an off-white color which gave their bedroom a spacious feeling. They did get a new mattress and boxspring along with new sheets, and pillows. Somehow Riley had managed to add a poster to each corner of the bed so they could create a canopy over the top. Both of them reassured me that it felt like a whole new set.

The best part of the move, however, was in the selling of Anne's house. She admitted that she had gone through some difficult moments sorting through memories of her past life with Frank. But, for the sake of her new relationship with Riley, she committed to doing so. The real estate agent continued to bring more and more people through the house. Finally, one woman returned again and again. She was always alone with the real estate agent and seemed very tentative. So Anne was surprised when the offer she got on the house was from her. When she questioned the agent, she was told that this woman was a recent widow, raising a son by herself. Anne couldn't help but see the parallel to her own life. They agreed on a selling price quickly and honorably. The woman, Elizabeth, wanted to come by on several occasions to check out certain measurements and features. Anne was happy to accommodate her and, before long, they had a comfortable relationship. Anne shared with Elizabeth her own story of being a widow in this house, raising a son by herself. Elizabeth's husband had died suddenly as well, so they could understand each other's specific pain.

Moving became a whole different event for Anne. She was delighted to leave her home to Elizabeth and her young son. Packing was easy from then on. She even left some of Nelson's bedroom furniture for Elizabeth's use. They remain in touch to this day. Anne was happy to turn over her home to her new friend, making her own transition easier.

Peggy

New life, new breath

Peggy had been living in the same townhouse for five years. It was small but ade-
quate. She had been married to a man twenty-five years her senior
who had recently died in the townhouse. At the age of 82, Will
simply didn't wake up one morning. Peggy was concerned about
whether she should have the townhouse blessed, having read somewhere that if someone dies in your house you're in big trouble.

Another issue that she was dealing with was her own health. Even
before Will died, she had been having asthma problems. There were
days when she couldn't breathe, and Will would have to take her to

the emergency room. She had gained weight and felt overwhelmed most of the time. She was beginning to wonder if there was something wrong with the place.

When we set up a time to have an appointment together, she was very adamant that when I got there I was *not* to enter through the front door. Instead there was a side door where everyone entered and that was where I was to go. She assured me that a lot of people find it confusing, but that's how they had set up the place. Knowing what I know about front doors, I was having some concerns about this arrangement already.

I arrived at her townhouse and, despite her clear instructions, I still felt confusion around the choice of doors. She came out of the side door (which she considers her front door) and met me. Peggy said she usually has to watch for people who are coming to visit so they can get directed to the "right" door.

I began my visit with Peggy by discussing the death of her husband. He had not been feeling well, but due to his age, Peggy hadn't been alarmed by that. A few days later, he had a heart attack in his sleep and died. She was grateful he didn't have to suffer. He had lived a full and productive life. They had traveled extensively during their marriage of twenty years. I suggested that if she wanted to clear the townhouse, she could do some very simple activities on her own. Or if she wanted my support, we could do one together. Taking a small bell and ringing it as she's walking through the space is one way to clear it. Holding a candle and walking through the townhouse is another way to cleanse. Incense would also work. Will's death wasn't violent nor had he suffered or struggled for an extended time. A cleansing in this case might feel more like a blessing. Peggy decided that she'd love to cleanse and bless the house with a bell, but it felt like something she'd rather do on her own privately.

We then turned to discussing the concept of the front door. In Feng Shui, front doors are considered the *mouth of ch'i*, meaning they're a passage for good luck and good fortune. When there's confusion around where the front door is located or when the door cannot be seen, these good-luck opportunities may be passing by. The front door needs to be obvious. Additionally, the front door should be a different color from anything else on the building. The preferred color is red or some variation of red, but any color will do as long as it's a color of choice by the owners. Peggy reminded me that she lives in a townhouse which would not allow her to paint her door. But she could put some pots of flowers on both sides of the door as well as a wind chime or a flag.

The bigger question at hand was why Peggy was not using her front door in the first place, requiring this awkward, confusing experience for anyone who came to her place. She showed me a bookshelf sitting in front of the front door. She needed additional space, so she blocked off the front door from the inside. The door couldn't be used even if she wanted to use it (see *Original Plan*).

Plus, when Peggy used the side door as her front door, the flow of ch'i or energy entered into her dining room. While eating food or having tea, the nutrition of the food can escape much too quickly out the "front door" leaving the people in the house with health problems. In addition, having the impact of a food-related activity greet her every time she came into her space set up additional food issues. There was a trigger for wanting to eat food whenever she would walk into her house. Peggy confirmed that she had gained an enormous amount of weight since moving in. But she also assured me that she never ate at the table, opting to eat on her coffee table while watching television. I assured her that actual use or non-use of the table didn't matter. The flow of the energy was still there.

Using the actual front door as the entrance to her space would be ideal. She'd be welcomed by her living room which is an appropriate greeting. There was a closet by the real front door in which to hang

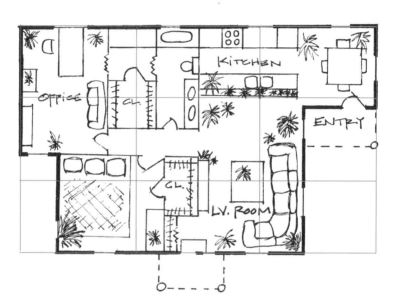

Original Plan

her coat which she didn't have by the side door. Of course, the question she expressed was where she was going to put her book shelf if she opened up her front door again.

From the size of Peggy's furniture and the amount of furniture she had, I guessed that she had moved from a much larger space. She confirmed that this was true. When she and Will moved to this townhouse, they were down-sizing from a four-bedroom house. Each of the bedrooms from the house was larger, yet they had tried to move as much as they could into this small townhouse. To say the space was overwhelming doesn't adequately describe the experience of being in this house.

The living room was small but not too small. The problem with the room was she had a sectional sofa which was too big for the space. Along with that, Peggy grew plants. Big ones. And lots of them. She was intentionally trying to create a cozy jungle feel, which I assured her she had created. But the room felt stifling. I couldn't breathe standing in the living room. Some of the plants were not doing well and needed pruning. Some of the plants simply needed to be removed. I was of the opinion that if most of the plants were removed, the large sectional could work. I also invited her to think about removing some of the sections of the sofa to minimize its impact and get this piece of furniture to be more in scale with the size of the room.

There was a half-wall between the living room and the kitchen. The top of the half-wall was a counter space with far too many plants and bric-a-brac. She was trying to create a barrier, but neither the living room nor the kitchen was big enough to introduce a barrier between them. Her kitchen was a small galley style with only one end open. Peggy needed light in there, not darkness. I suggested a mirror behind her stovetop to not only bring in light but to reflect what was happening behind her back. She had limited counter space, but almost every square inch was covered. No wonder she was having trouble seeing her future. Again I suggested simplicity.

Peggy used the back bedroom as a home office. She wrote letters and paid bills in this room, but otherwise didn't spend much time in there. A gas fireplace was on one wall. She would turn it on if she was ever in the room for any length of time.

The front bedroom was where she slept. Peggy and Will had moved their king-sized bed into a room that could not accommodate such a large piece of furniture. The room was wall-to-wall bed. There was hardly any space to move around. One side of the bed was up against the wall. The only free corner had a huge palm tree reaching out towards the bed. A walk-in closet off this bedroom housed a dresser and an over-abundance of clothes, many of them her late husband's.

At this point, Peggy and I decided to sit down to determine how she wanted to live her life now that she was alone. She told me that a life insurance settlement had left her with considerable money, but she wasn't yet ready to move. The thought of moving felt daunting to her right now, so she simply wanted to improve the conditions here in the townhouse. We discussed the fact that Feng Shui views the back of a space as private. This is where the bedrooms and the kitchen should be located. Her bedroom was in the front of the house. "Was there any way she could trade her office for her bedroom?" I asked. Bring the office to the front of the townhouse and put her bed in a safe back corner. I also suggested she down-size her bed. She agreed she was ready to do that. It felt too lonely sleeping in such a large bed without Will.

To me this was a crucial place to start. Her son lived in the area and had offered to help her in any way. It seemed to me her asthma could likely be linked to the over-sized furniture as well as the overwhelming amount of plants and other items. It was no wonder she couldn't catch her breath. I strongly urged her to reconsider all the plants and determine which ones she really wanted to have in her home.

Peggy kept me posted as things started to happen. She and her son spent many days cleaning out and moving furniture. Peggy's asthma seemed to get progressively worse as they shuffled things around.

Twice in one day he rushed her to an emergency room because she couldn't breathe. She still insisted on continuing with the project, thinking her condition was related somehow to the condition of the townhouse. I finally returned about two months after our initial visit to see what had happened. She wanted further advice.

The front door was still blocked when I got there, but the amount of work that had happened in the two bedrooms was astounding (see *Phase I*). Her son had painted both of the rooms as long as they were moving everything out. Her bedroom was a soft lavender—her favorite color. It was also appropriate, considering the bedroom was in the Wealth area of her space. She had found a double bed, which allowed the dresser from the walk-in closet to be moved into this room. Peggy had only one large plant in the bedroom despite her inclination to move in a bunch more.

The front bedroom had been transformed into an office. Basically everything stayed as it was in the back room. The room was painted a beautiful periwinkle blue. I suggested a mirror over her gas fireplace to balance the fire and to correct the missing corner in her Knowledge area. A mirror will expand a space and "move" a wall. I also asked about changing the hinges on the closet door so it wouldn't keep bumping into the door to the room. These create an

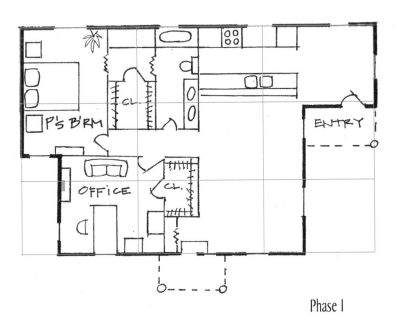

P's B'RM

CL.

OFFICE

CL.

ENTRY

Phase I

195

"arguing" vibration. By changing the door on the closet, she would be reflecting more harmony in her life.

Peggy had moved a fold-out couch into the room that was now the office. When I asked her about its use, she realized she never had overnight company. There was no use for it anymore. She hadn't thought about whether she should dispose of it or not. I suggested she give it away or sell it. "Funny," she commented. When she and her son were moving the fold-out couch, he had off-handedly said when she didn't want it anymore he could use it. She commented to me how blind she had gotten with regard to her possessions. It hadn't occurred to her to let it go. My point in letting it go was now she would have a place for her bookshelf standing in front of the front door.

Before we left the office, she showed me the walk-in closet which had been made into a storage area. Then she showed me her closet off her bedroom. It had required sorting through clothes, memories, and treasures. During this sorting process, Peggy had had one of the worst asthma attacks she'd ever endured. But the sorting got done and she was very relieved. In fact, in the last few weeks she'd hardly had any trouble with asthma at all.

All of this cleaning and sorting had spilled out into the living room as well. Even though there were still a lot of plants, many of them had been removed. She had given some of them to friends and neighbors.

Because she never used her front door, Peggy had positioned the furniture accordingly. If she were to begin using the door, she would need to look at re-arranging things. She shared with me that deep down she didn't want the television in the living room as she couldn't overcome the temptation to watch it. She found herself over-eating while staring at some program she didn't even care about. And she felt she could make better use of her time if she wasn't tempted to turn it on. We explored the possibility of removing it altogether, moving it into the office which she could make into a den, or getting a cabinet with doors on the front so that it wouldn't be so prominent in the room.

Peggy really liked the idea of putting it in a cabinet with doors. But she resonated more with moving it into the office. She could see the value in re-defining the office as a den since she didn't use the desk more than an hour a week. Maybe she'd need the fold-out couch after all!

The other issue Peggy wanted to discuss was her kitchen. Not much had happened there. I suggested she remove every single item, plant and bric-a-brac off the top of the divider wall and leave it empty for nine days. I wanted her to experience that feeling for a time. Then she could replace whatever items she thought she'd like to have there. She also wanted further explanation of the mirror behind the stove. She wasn't sure she'd like that, watching herself cook and all. But, she had a mirror in her storage area which she brought out and propped behind the stove to see how it might look. The point of the mirror, as I reinforced with Peggy, was to bring more light into the darkness of the kitchen and to reflect the world going on behind her. She'd give it a try.

As I was leaving, she handed me a plant! I assured her I'd give it a good home. Along with that she asked to set up another appointment. Two months later I returned.

You can imagine my surprise and delight (see *Phase 2*) when I pulled up to Peggy's townhouse where I saw two planters of red flowers standing on either side of the new front door! The door was open and Peggy was ready to greet me when I got out of my car. She looked fabulous and I told her so. A friend of hers was taking her to an aerobics class for seniors, and she had to admit she was starting to feel better about herself. Although no weight had been lost yet, she could feel a distinct difference in her body.

She had waited for me to help her arrange her living room furniture. I couldn't help but notice the television was gone. She'd given it away! Every single plant had been removed, and all trace of plants was gone from the top of the half-wall. She confided that, when the last of the plants had been moved out, her asthma seemed to have moved out as well. She was hoping to incorporate a few plants here and there but was waiting for some input from me. The most stunning change was

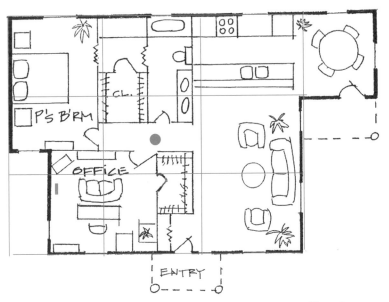

CL.

P'S B'RM

OFFICE

ENTRY

Phase 2

Peggy had gotten rid of the sectional and had replaced it with a small sofa and two chairs. The furniture was perfectly scaled to the room, yet still big enough for comfort.

Before we began moving furniture around, Peggy wanted to show me the office, which was no longer just an office. She had kept her fold-out couch and had created a cozy little space for herself. She had replaced her large desk with a smaller one. The bookshelf fit in perfectly. And in the corner was a small television for those times when she wanted to watch something. The television hardly made an impact on the room as it was small and in a little cabinet with closed doors. An Oriental rug tied the whole room together. A fountain kept the ch'i flowing. Besides her bedroom, this had become her favorite room, and I could see why.

It wasn't hard to let the furniture find its proper place in the living room. We found a couple areas where a plant would be the perfect touch, much to Peggy's delight. I suggested a round coffee table at some point, as it would be a nice message of harmony and cooperation to her. If she was open to it, I also suggested a round table in the dining area for the same reasons. Peggy had reluctantly removed all the clutter from the divider wall to discover after only a couple of days she really liked the look. Things felt quieter and less hectic. She decided to put nothing back, leaving it clear of all items.

Because the front door was no longer in the extension in Partnership, the bagua needed to be adjusted accordingly. Based on the new bagua, we located the exact center of Peggy's space (●), which was in the hallway. She opted to hang a wind chime denoting this spot that she could ring as she walked back and forth in her hall. Her intention was to "call in" good health and a balanced life.

Two years later, Peggy continues to live in her townhouse. She is always working on her clutter tendency. Her asthma remains a challenge. When her space starts to feel too stifling for her due to clutter, she notices that her asthma is more acute. She finds it endearing when her space can't breathe, neither can she. Peggy's space reflects her life.

In the two years since she began her journey with Feng Shui, she has lost over twenty pounds. As with her space and her asthma, Peggy's weight issue is a continual process. Overeating had become another form of clutter in her life.

Antoinette

Is it time to go?

Antoinette and I stood in the middle of her
living room—or rather what would be her
living room. Antoinette had lived in her three-bedroom rambler for
23 years. Most of that time she had lived there as a single parent to
her daughter. She divorced her husband five years after moving in,
when her daughter was three.

Antoinette had been very entrepreneurial and successful over the
years. Though she had made considerable money as a commercial real
estate agent, she chose to stay in the same small home, providing her
daughter and herself with stability. In the last couple of years, she had
begun an immense remodeling program.

The first phase involved new plumbing, a new furnace, and new wiring throughout the house. She was ready to move to more visible improvements at the point of our consultation. She was putting on an addition to the back of her house providing her with a family room. She was changing one of her bedrooms into a large walk-in closet off the master bedroom. Her daughter, Jamie, had graduated and was living elsewhere so Antoinette was converting that bedroom into a guest room. Plus, she was remodeling her bathroom. While all the hardwood floors were being redone on the main floor, she had moved herself into the basement. Antoinette called me to go over her plans in case there was something she needed to change or reconsider.

We started in her bedroom since that holds so much importance in Feng Shui. We discussed where she would situate her bed once the floors were completed. We determined there was easily enough room to put the bed in the command corner of the room. Sleeping in the corner furthest from the entrance to the room is considered a very strong and commanding spot. Being there would enable Antoinette to feel safe and secure, therefore she should be able to sleep better.

We also located the center of her house where Antoinette assured me she would hang a round, faceted crystal (●) for balance and harmony. The ramifications of adding on a family room in the back of her house happened to be a blessing for her. Measuring the proposed new

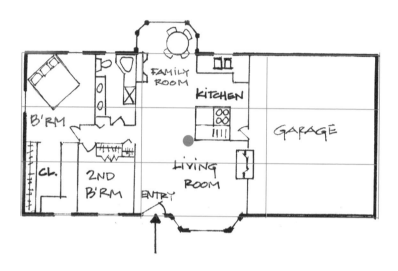

addition, we could determine it was less than half of the full width of her home, thus making it a nice extension in the Wealth and Fame and Reputation areas. This could assure her continued success at work.

Antoinette also wanted me to see her garage where her Partnership area was located. I couldn't help but laugh as she succinctly described the area as "full of dead wood." She confirmed any attempts at igniting a new relationship in her life had not succeeded.

She decided cleaning out the garage would be something to do if she really wanted a new partner.

It was a year later when Antoinette called me again. Things had changed. Her daughter had moved back in, for one thing, and Antoinette was now ready to remodel her kitchen. Jamie had graduated from college and hadn't yet decided on a job. Even though Antoinette wanted to support her daughter, she didn't want her to get overly settled and never embark on her own journey.

The guest room was now converted back to Jamie's space. I assured Antoinette that the position of that room was a good decision since it was in the front of the house and close to the front door. These factors are conducive to moving someone along on their way.

The kitchen was being totally redesigned. Antoinette was open to rearranging the appliances to provide a better cooking experience. She was adding a dishwasher and installing all new cabinetry. She expressed her reluctance to tear up the house again but she really hated her kitchen. Her feelings were affecting her eating habits. She hardly ever cooked anymore even though it used to be one of her favorite pastimes. She either ate out or brought home takeout food. She wanted to get back to cooking healthy meals again, since restaurant food had been dramatically affecting her weight.

Is it time to go?

Due to the small size of the kitchen, as well as the dark cabinets, flooring, and countertops, she knew the kitchen had to lighten up. Antoinette was planning to install a skylight over the stove to get some light. I urged her to reconsider this idea, as adding a skylight to an existing building was similar to a puncture wound or a bullet hole. A skylight would "bleed" the energy out of her space and out of her life. Adding it above the stove allowed any nourishment from food she may be preparing to escape as well. She decided then and there to forego the skylight and instead enlarge the window over the sink.

We sketched out possible kitchen layouts. We didn't want the stovetop and the sink directly opposite one another—fire and water don't mix (the stove being fire and the sink having water energy), nor did we want the stovetop and refrigerator right next to one another (again fire—the stove, and water—the refrigerator, not mixing). Unfortunately, no matter what Antoinette did in the kitchen, it was still small. Designing the cabinets, flooring, and countertops to be light in color was the only way she could see to expand the area.

The walk-in closet off her bedroom was well-designed and efficient. Antoinette loved her bedroom area and assured me she was sleeping well. Her bathroom was exquisite. She had incorporated a whirlpool tub, all new tile, and a unique use of glass block around the shower.

The family room addition in back was her all-time favorite room, however. The experience of being in the room was a dramatic shift from the rest of her house. The ceilings were high and vaulted. There were large windows on two sides overlooking her backyard. A gas fireplace added a coziness to the room despite its sense of expansion. A small round table enabled Antoinette to eat in there, while two big comfy chairs provided close scrutiny and benefit of the fireplace. She loved the spaciousness, the windows, the light. I was beginning to wonder why Antoinette was working so hard to make this little rambler work for her. Its small windows and low ceilings didn't seem to suit her style.

Antoinette shared with me that the last phase of her remodeling had gone way over budget. She had impeccable taste and had incorporated only top quality products and first-class workmanship—down to custom drawer pulls in the bathroom and custom-mixed floor stain throughout the house. All of these options had driven the expense up considerably. Although money was not a major issue for her, she was still wincing from the cost of the project and was trying not to let the kitchen remodeling get out of hand.

The dead wood had been cleaned out of the garage. One of Antoinette's neighbors was happy to take it off her hands to use in his fireplace. However, once the wood had been removed, the floor swept and scrubbed, she saw how badly the garage floor had settled over the years. It actually sloped toward the house. This, of course, explained the mystery water that would appear in her basement on occasion. She saw this as just another major project for the future, much to her disappointment.

Six months passed before Antoinette called me to come to her house again. As I pulled up to her house for the third time, I couldn't help but notice that from the outside the house was still a small, unassuming rambler on a street lined with similar houses. Once inside, of course, it was evident a tremendous amount of work had occurred. But from the outside, the place gave no indication of the transformation. It was still a small house.

The kitchen was now completed and her daughter had vacated the space to take a job on the east coast. Antoinette was now considering her options for the garage. As before, when I saw the finished results of her construction, I could sense the care and deliberation with which she had chosen each and every item. The kitchen was everything she had dreamed and hoped for. The front bedroom was again a lovely guest room furnished with priceless antiques which she had inherited from her family.

Since my last visit, Antoinette had sold her share of a partnership with which she'd been associated for over ten years. She was starting her own company, at home, working off her old kitchen table in the family room. In light of that, she had decided to tear down the whole garage that was sloping and re-build a newer and slightly bigger one with an office in the back.

Antoinette made it clear she was not at all excited about this kind of project—the expense and the disruption—but she felt she had no other choice. She hated how her new business was expanding itself all over her beautiful family room. She couldn't relax in there anymore because her work was a constant reminder. Since the room had not been set up as an office, files were everywhere. There were no provisions for storage, so things were stacked on the floor, the table, and even on the comfy chairs. To get better organized, Antoinette felt as though she'd have to live through one more remodeling project. By having an office in the back of the garage, she could set things up the way she wanted and get it all out of her family room. She looked tired just thinking about it.

I decided to go out on a limb. "Would it be easier for you to move?" Antoinette looked a little astonished. She admitted that she hadn't thought about it. The house had always been her domain. Leaving it seemed somehow scary. "Why don't you ask the house what you should do?" I said. I could tell from her expression that she thought I was kidding. When she saw I was serious, she said, "How would that work?" I explained to her one effective way she could connect with her house would be to write it a letter. Antoinette's logical mind was struggling. "And say what? And am I supposed to believe the house would write back?" "Let's try connecting with it right now," I suggested.

"Pretend your house has personified itself for a moment and it is sitting in this empty chair," I said, pointing to the one empty chair around her table. "You've just told it you're going to tear down the garage and rebuild a new one that will have an office for you. What's the first thing the house would say to you?"

Antoinette exploded without a moment's hesitation: "What are you? Stupid? Stop trying to make me into a Cadillac when I'm just a little Pinto. I'll never be what you want. You've outgrown me. You outgrew me years ago. I will never live up to your expectations. I've appreciated what you've done to me, but you need to move, girl. You'll be happier and I'll be happier. All these remodeling projects are as tiring on me as they are on you."

Antoinette stopped. She had tears in her eyes. She sat quietly for a few minutes, wiping her eyes. "Is this for real?" I assured her it was more than real. Her answers were from her heart, not from her head. After a few minutes she asked, "Now what?"

I suggested she just be with the idea for awhile. Let the garage project rest and see how she was feeling in a week or so. To support her clarity around this issue, we again pinpointed the center of her house. Although she had intended to do so after my first visit, Antoinette committed to hanging a round, faceted crystal in this spot. Meanwhile, I also recommended she convert the guest room to a temporary office. This would enable her to reclaim her family room which she so loved. Because the guest room was small and had only one little window, she had never considered using it for anything other than a bedroom. I suggested she look upon this shift as temporary headquarters for her office. She could still take her cordless phone or her laptop computer out to the family room so she could enjoy the view. But she would have a place for files and storage that would enable her to have a sense of order. It would also buy her some time while she considered whether or not she would actually move.

Antoinette called me several times to process her thoughts. She had been out looking at other places, unsure of what she was even looking for. After a couple of months, she decided moving seemed appropriate. Her daughter thought it was a great idea as well. I suggested that she write down all the features she wanted in a new space so when she went looking she could check her list. One piece of information she had never consciously acknowledged was having a yard with the required upkeep was too much work. Although she liked to garden, it wasn't a passion. This alone opened up a lot more possibilities for her; she was now considering a townhouse.

Is it time to go?

The next time I heard from Antoinette, her house was on the market. She had made an offer on a townhouse overlooking the river. It was big and spacious and light! It had the features she was trying to create in her small house. I wasn't surprised her house sold quickly. Before she moved, I returned one final time to do a closing ceremony with Antoinette. It felt important that, after all these years, she spend some time expressing gratitude to the house for its security and shelter. We spent an hour together one afternoon while she verbalized to me the memories she had of her home. Some of her memories were nostalgic and a little sad, some were happy and touching. She wanted to leave the home clear of any negativity for the young couple who was moving in and expecting their first baby in a few months.

Antoinette had me come to her new townhouse after she had gotten settled. It goes without saying she looked like a different person. She now had room to blossom and expand. She was cooking again, for herself and for her friends. A new relationship seemed to be in the works.

A few months after Antoinette moved, I received a call from a couple who wanted me to come and look at their home. It seems Antoinette had given them my name and number. You guessed it-they were living in Antoinette's old house. And thus we began all over again.

Marilyn and Don

Finding the new in the old

Marilyn and Don called me on the recom-
mendation of some friends. They were about to finalize a deal on
their current house and within the month would be closing on
another house they wanted to buy. They thought some Feng Shui
advice at this stage would be a good idea.

I met them at the new place to look around. Although it was
empty, the house still exuded a lot of charm and beauty. I could see
why they were drawn to it. Nevertheless, I am at a distinct disadvantage when I have to look at an empty space since I can't see firsthand
what people own and where they're going to position things. However, they were able to describe to me in great detail the various
pieces of furniture they had and where they envisioned placing them.

Finding the new in the old

I asked about the predecessor and whether they knew why the house was being sold. Marilyn and Don were buying it from a young widow whose husband had had a fatal heart attack while watching television at home one evening. She chose not to stay in the house after his death. As they were relaying this story to me, I noticed a missing corner in the Partnership area of this house. I pointed this out to them and discussed what they might do to minimize the impact from this feature. I also spoke to them about the impact of having someone die in the space. The widow had told them a family minister had been out to bless the house before she put it on the market. Both Marilyn and Don felt as though this was sufficient action.

Of the two of them, Don was by far the more excited about this new place. At least he was outwardly expressing his enthusiasm more than Marilyn. He was quick to show me all the features he was going to like about this new home. He could see his workbench in one area of the basement and his recliner by the window. He loved that the garage was attached, unlike their current home. Actually, there wasn't much Don didn't like about this house.

Marilyn was more subdued. "What's your favorite feature?" I finally asked her. She shrugged, surprised at my question. "I like it all," she said noncommittally. "Is there one room you like most of all?" I pursued. "They're all fine," she assured me. "Are you thinking of painting any of the rooms?" Marilyn clearly hadn't thought about it. While she was pondering the question, Don jumped in with the answers. Painting was definitely in the plan. In fact, it was so elaborate and dramatic, I found it interesting that Marilyn didn't know about it. When he was done describing the painting plans, I turned to Marilyn and asked, "Are you okay with that?" "Sure," she said flatly.

Something was going on here. Synchronistically, Don got a call on his cell phone. The connection wasn't very good so he was having to shout into the phone. He stepped outside so we wouldn't be disturbed. I looked at Marilyn. "Are you happy about this move?" I kept my voice low. Marilyn looked me straight in the eyes and said, "Look, if Don's happy, I'm happy." That wasn't what I'd asked her. "Do you even like this place?" "It's okay," she said. "Do you like your old house better?" I guessed. Marilyn's eyes filled with tears. "I love the house we're in. It breaks my heart to think of leaving it. But Don wants to move. He's sure that if I get in here, I'll learn to love this place, too."

Don came back inside. Marilyn reached for a tissue. I stared at their missing piece in Partnership. We talked about a few more ideas for floor coverings before my time was up. Marilyn and Don estimated that they would be closing on their current house within the week, two at the most. The closing date for the new place hadn't been set yet, but they were hopeful it could occur a day or two before.

Before we left one another that day, we arranged another appointment for me to return, giving them a few weeks to settle in. As a parting thought, I suggested that they hang a ceramic wind chime in the Partnership area of their current home. I figured that they could begin activating the energy of their Partnership in their old home, in anticipation of moving into a place where it would be challenged. In my own mind, I speculated that in energizing the relationship between the two of them, Marilyn might find her own voice to speak up about her wishes. Sometimes activating the energy in an area can bring a situation to the surface and force a shift. They both assured me that they could hang a wind chime for the remaining days in their space.

One week after our initial visit, Don called me. The anxiety in his voice was evident. It seems that Marilyn had let him know that she didn't want to move. The night after they hung their wind chime she had erupted during supper. Don had been taken off guard, for he hadn't noticed her sadness whenever they talked about the new place.

But that wasn't all. While the two of them were discussing the situation over dinner, the real estate agent called to say the people who were supposed to buy their home didn't qualify. The closing was off. Because their current home wasn't selling, they could not move forward with the closing on the new house. Financially, Marilyn and Don were in no position to maintain ownership on two houses. Everything was off. They wouldn't be moving any time soon. He thought the events had been arranged so carefully, he said. He couldn't figure out what had happened. Coincidentally things seemed to fall apart once the wind chime got in place. Did I have any ideas?

I supported them leaving the wind chime in place. I assured Don that there was always a bigger plan and to trust that everything was going as it should. He speculated that the only good he could see in this turn of events was that he wasn't going to have to clean off his desk in order to move.

He couldn't hide his disappointment, although he certainly didn't want to leave a house that Marilyn felt so strongly about. Evidently, over the years of their marriage, some patterns of dysfunctional communication had settled in, he admitted. He was certain he knew his wife well and knew what was best for both of them. But during one eventful dinner he found that he didn't know her well at all. For this, he felt badly. He wanted me to come to their current home. They were having to re-group.

Until I could get there, I suggested that Don proceed with his plans to clean off his desk. Horizontal surfaces hold the potential for vision and creativity. The more a surface is cluttered and filled, the less vision is available. Clearing the top of his work space could bring him some clarity and insight that he wanted, not to mention creativity. He agreed to do so.

When I arrived at Marilyn and Don's house, they were sitting on their porch. Again, the two of them walked me around the space, but this time Marilyn actively participated in the conversation. She clearly was invested in the house. Don, too, shared some fond memories of the space. Their wind chime was still in place. Don still maintained that the wind chime had something to do with their change in direction. He tried to put a positive spin on the situation by admitting that maybe moving into a place where a man had just died and where there were potential Partnership problems was not such a good thing.

I asked him what his biggest disappointment was about? He was sad about the workbench area. And he really hated not having an attached garage. In the house they were living in, he saw no options to attach a garage. Ultimately Don had perceived the move to a different home as a symbol of a new beginning for Marilyn and him.

When we entered the office, Don was quick to excuse the look of his desk. He hadn't cleaned it off yet. Without the urgency of a move, he had lost heart and didn't tackle it. He didn't see the point. I wanted to re-frame the activity of cleaning off the desk so that it became more than just a task. I suggested he consider the busyness of creating space on his desk like finding the answer to whether they should begin looking for another home or stay in their present one. By cleaning it off, he might find a creative solution for them. "Like some remodel plans for an addition?" he asked jokingly. "You might be surprised," I teased him.

Their house was basically a rectangular home with a detached garage out in back. I could see why they might want to start over because most of the decorating (wallpaper, carpet, paint) needed updating. Marilyn admitted it had been over twenty years since they had fixed up any of the rooms. I made many suggestions, trying to prioritize what I felt would be the most impactful for them. I didn't want them to get discouraged, but something needed to shift. At the top of the list was Don's desk. Somehow that felt important—probably because he was resisting it the most. This time Don promised he would most certainly clean the desk looking for the "answer" to their problem.

I also got them focused on their bedroom, believing that if they could update the room of intimacy and rejuvenation, it would affect all other aspects of their lives. We spent some time brainstorming about favorite colors, themes, and new furniture. Marilyn looked like new life had been breathed into her.

Two weeks later. Don called. "You won't believe this," he started. "I cleaned off my desk and in one of the stacks was a house plan I had torn out of a magazine years ago. I kept it because it had an idea for

219

an addition onto the back of a house that looked a lot like ours. We've already spoken to a contractor about the possibility of adding onto our house. With the equity we've acquired over the years, we're going to proceed. You were right. The answer was on my desk all along."

Don elaborated on the details, describing how, by tearing down the old garage, they could rebuild a new one off the kitchen. The garage would be large enough to have a workshop area in it. His enthusiasm came through loud and clear. Marilyn was relieved and delighted. They wanted to set up an appointment so I could look at their proposed plans to see if there might be any problems or concerns.

But that wasn't all. Don had another matter to discuss. He asked if I had heard the news about the house that burned down a week or so ago. It seems there was an electrical fire that completely burned down a house in the northeast part of town. I told him I had heard something about it but hadn't paid a lot of attention to the story. The fire took place in the middle of the night. It was considered a total loss. Don's voice tensed. That was the house they had planned to buy! Luckily, the new owners weren't home at the time of the fire, but Marilyn and Don might not have been as fortunate. The big plan had definitely been at work for them.

Before hanging up, Don said to me: "How does this stuff work? This Feng Shui stuff? It seems like you do something unrelated to what you're trying to work on and it unfolds something else. You hang a wind chime and it saves your life. You clean your desk and you add a garage." "Yeah, that's about how it works," I responded. "Just keep your wind chime in place and keep your desk clear and you'll be okay, Don." There was no argument with him on that account.

The stories never end even though, at this moment, the book does. I believe we learn from stories and from watching other people. All of these personal chronicles, or parts of them, could be any one of us. We are all working to reach our fullest potential and looking to find ways to ease through difficulties.

It is my hope that you will find some piece or two to take away for implementation in your own life. Perhaps one of the situations reminded you of your particular story. Trying even the smallest adjustment in Feng Shui can bring about some awesome shifts. I trust that in my telling these stories, you can see how to create your own experience of living Feng Shui.

—Carole J. Hyder

Glossary

A

Arrows, Poison – *See* Poison Arrows.

Aquariums – Often used in an area where things feel "stuck." The gentle flow of the water and the movement of the fish can enhance money if placed in the Wealth area of the bagua. The water element of an aquarium can also off-set the effects of "burn out" from a fireplace, if placed on or near the hearth. If an aquarium requires too much time to maintain, a picture of fish or a sculptural fish piece (i.e., dolphins) would also work.

B

Bagua – A mental map determining the placement of nine life issues in a home, on the lot or a garden, over a desk or on a bed. When a bagua is appropriately placed and enhanced, your life begins to manifest good fortune and blessed occurrences. The nine areas are Career, Knowledge, Family, Wealth, Fame & Reputation, Partnership, Children & Creativity, Helpful People and Health.

Beams – Can be divisive between a family or between business relationships. They should either be removed completely, if possible, or painted the same color as the ceiling to minimize their impact. If the beams can neither be removed nor painted, avoid sitting under a beam at your desk or in your favorite chair. And avoid lying under a beam when in bed by simply moving the bed.

Bed – One of the three most important pieces of furniture in a home. (*See* Desk and Stove.) The bed should be positioned so that it is in the command position of the bedroom. (*See* Command Position.) When lying in bed, the occupant must be able to

225

see the entrance to the room. It is important that there be nothing stored under the bed and that there be an adequate, solid headboard on the bed. There should be sufficient space around both sides of the bed to get in and out either side, representing more options in life. The bagua can be superimposed over a bed orientating the foot of the bed as the front of the bagua. When working with the bagua on a bed, the energy or ch'i around an issue can be changed by intentionally placing items between the mattress and the box-springs of the bed.

Bedroom, Guest – The closer to the front of the house, the less likely guests will stay long. Guest rooms can serve additional functions, like being a part-time office, an exercise room or sewing room. Guest rooms can also be located in the lower level, near the front door or over a garage without serious consequences.

Bedroom, Master – Ideally in the back of the home. The bedroom should not be over a garage, near the front door or at the end of a long hallway. Bedroom should not be cluttered with television, computer, books, pictures of family or friends or exercise equipment. Master bedroom should ideally be in a command position of the house. (*See* Command Position).

Bells – Can be used to "call in" an intention. Hung near a back door that falls in the Wealth area of the house, a bell can slow down the quick exit of money. A bell can be hung on a doorknob or near a front door to act as a form of protection to those who work or live there. It is important that the bell have a pleasant sound to the occupant and not be a source of irritation when it rings.

Birdbaths – *See* Ponds.

Blocked Entry – A wall or structure that impedes someone from walking straight ahead into a space. A mirror or a print or painting with a dimensional feeling will "open up" the space. Creating the illusion of space keeps the energy flowing.

Bookshelves – Whether at home or in an office, need to be kept in order. Shelving should ideally only be waist-high in an office so as not to feel overwhelmed when seated at a desk or in a chair. If shelves go higher than eye level, then keep the upper shelves "light." The use of plants, artwork, or photos can soften the impact of tall shelving. A library would naturally have tall book shelves which are acceptable, yet they still need to be kept in order, with current books, eliminating outdated information. (*See* Library.)

C

Candles – Can be used to "enlighten" a space or get "enlightenment" around an issue. The intentional lighting of a candle brings illumination, both physically and mentally.

Career – One of the nine areas of the bagua that represents the activities and directions for your pursuits in life. It is represented by the color black.

Ch'i – Universal energy. Feng Shui works with enhancing and manipulating the flow of ch'i in a space or an environment.

Children & Creativity – One of the nine areas of the bagua that includes anything which you may "birth" in life, in addition to children—a book, a thesis, poetry, music, business, etc.

Clocks – In order for your life to keep "ticking" along, all displayed clocks need to work. A malfunctioning clock can give a message that something else in life is also not working.

Clutter – Too many items in a space causing unclear thinking and feelings of overwhelm and exhaustion. Clutter can be unspecified piles of paper, magazines, newspapers or it can be unused clothes in the closet. It can be unfinished projects, too, many books or collections of items.

Colors – An option for adjusting energy in a space. Colors should be used that are liked by all members of the family or business. Each area of the bagua has a color connected to it which can be used in its pure form or any shade or tint of it:

    Career – Black
    Knowledge – Blue
    Family – Green

    Wealth – Purple
    Fame & Reputation – Red
    Partnership – Pink
    Children & Creativity – White
    Helpful People – Gray
    Health – Yellow

Command Position – Back corner of a space at the greatest angle from the entrance door. A command position establishes ownership and control in the space. It is ideal if the master bedroom can be in the command position in a house, or if a bed can be in the command position in the bedroom.

Creativity – *See* Children & Creativity.

Crystals – A round, faceted crystal acts as a barrier when too much ch'i comes down a hallway; it balances out distortion or unevenness; a crystal can bring about clarity and calm a sense of overwhelm. A round faceted crystal can also infuse a space or a situation with a gentle movement where previously there was stagnation. A crystal hung in the center of a space can bring overall balance. It is more effective if the crystal is hung with a thread, string or fishline that has been cut 9 or 18 inches long.

Cul-de-Sac – Might be a potential for stagnation and a challenge for moving ahead. A house or business that is situated in a cul-de-sac is a recipient of the "dead end" of the road's flow. There appears to be nowhere to go. A small island in the middle of the turn-around would effectively direct the flow to keep on track and not allow it to puddle in the center. But often, this is not possible, so the individual spaces could make adjustments to assure the continuance of flow and movement by installing a fountain in front of the establishment or home, by hanging a

wind chime in front of the entrance, by having a spinning weather vane on top of the house or building, or by having a small, ornamental windmill by the front door.

D

Dead End – *See* Cul-de-Sac.

Desk – One of the three most important pieces of furniture. (*See* Bed and Stove.) The desk can hold a message of creativity and productivity or stagnation and heaviness depending on the amount of clutter stored on it. A desk would ideally be placed in the command position in an office (*see* Command Position) with the chair supported by a wall. Additionally, the desk should be positioned so that when seated at the desk, a person would easily see the entrance to the office. If there are no options in the office and a person must sit with their back to the entrance, then a small mirror positioned so that the desk's occupant can easily see behind them would be helpful. The desk should be appropriately sized to the proportion of the person using the desk. The bagua can be oriented over a desk with the front edge of the desk being the front of the bagua.

Door, Arguing – When two doors hit up against each other while trying to open or close either of them. If possible, change the hinges of one of the doors so that it opens another way to prevent the two from clashing. Arguing doors implies some argumentation in the space between those who live or work there.

Door, Back – Important to maintain the "flow" in life. A back door allows energy to come in and go out. The only problem area is if the back door falls in the Wealth area of the bagua. A wind chime either inside or outside the door will counteract money coming in the front door but going out the back door too quickly. It is important to always have a back door somewhere in the space. If there isn't one, a full-length mirror hung somewhere in the space (just not in Wealth) can represent the energy flow of a back door.

A back door should not be lined up directly with the front door as too much energy or ch'i can rush through the space. A front-door/back-door alignment indicates lost opportunities. Something physical needs to be placed between the two doors, like a screen, a plant, a round faceted crystal, curtains on the back door, a piece of furniture, etc. A back door should also not be in the Wealth area of the house as it is too easy for money to escape. Placing a bell or wind chime near a back door in

Wealth can ease the rush of finances out the door.

Door, Front – Often called the "mouth of ch'i" since it is the place through which opportunities arrive into a space. A front door should be the first feature to be seen when arriving at a home or office. It helps if it's a stand-alone color and does not match shutters, trim or shingles. If the front door is not used often due to an attached garage or a garage in the back of the house, it is advisable that the occupants or owners use the door on a regular basis to activate the ch'i around it. If the doorbell doesn't work, there is an indication that someone in the space is not being heard or acknowledged. All doorbells should work and be pleasant to hear.

Driveway – *See* Roads.

E

Elements – *See* Five Elements.

Energy – *See* Ch'i.

Extensions – A small protrusion from the main part of the house or room that measures less than half the full width of the space. An extension is auspicious and gives extra energy to the corresponding area of the bagua. Extensions do not need to be adjusted or changed in any way. Although the bagua does not directly include an extension in its layout, the extension is still part of the space and needs to be kept in order.

F

Fame & Reputation – One of the nine areas of the bagua representing your image and how the world sees you. It represents your integrity within the community and recognition. The color represented by this area is red.

Family – One of the nine areas of the bagua including members of your family of origin—parents, siblings, cousins and relations, as well as anyone you would consider part of your extended family. The color of the Family area is green.

Feng Shui – An ancient Chinese art of placement, literally translated as "wind" and "water."

Fireplace – Can often create too much fire, burning up the energy around health, money or career. The fireplace can be modified by adding some water elements to its surroundings, like a fountain, an aquarium, a picture of water or a seascape above the mantel, a picture of fish or a boat, or a mirror.

Five Elements – Fire, earth, metal, water, wood. The Five Elements are phases in nature that interact in constructive or dominating cycles. These five elements make up all that exists in the Universe. How the elements interact with one another determines the balance or imbalance in nature, in our spaces and in our lives.

Flowers – Fresh or silk flowers are appropriate. Fresh flowers need to be carefully monitored as they are already dying. As soon as they begin to wilt, it is important to remove them immediately. Silk flowers can be used as an alternative, keeping them clean and dust-free. Dried flowers should not be used as a Feng Shui adjustment at all unless they have some poignant or sensitive connection to you, like a dried wedding bouquet.

Fountains – Add water, movement and sound to an environment. Fountains are good for getting things moving or flowing again. They need to have clear, fresh water on a regular basis along with a total clean-out once a month to keep the flow going.

Furnace – Provides too much fire when in the center of a space, causing "burn out." Placing a small mirror face down on top of the furnace or the duct work tempers the impact of the fire energy. The mirror stays there indefinitely.

G

Garages – Should be kept in order and clean. Although usually a functional place to store cars, a garage may well be part of the bagua if it is attached to the house. Keeping things in order and swept out is a good activity to do if the garage is attached. Garages are more problematic if positioned in the front of the house, blocking the attention intended for the front door. The garage doors should be the same color as the rest of the house to allow the front door more notice. Just because a garage may not be attached to the house, there is still reason to keep a detached garage in order, since it is still on the property and is storing or holding possessions in your life.

H

Headboard – Represents support for the individuals sleeping in the bed. An ideal headboard is solid and comes up higher than the pillows. It should be attached directly to the bed frame and be sturdy enough to lean up against.

Health – One of the nine areas of the bagua representing physical, mental, emotional and spiritual well-being. The Health area is in the middle of a space. It is the core or hub around which life revolves. It is critical that this area be addressed for overall balance in life. The color for Health is yellow.

Helpful People – One of the nine areas of the bagua representing those people who can support you emotionally or financially. They might be a best friend, a relative, a minister, a plumber, a realtor or a travel agent. The color for Helpful People is gray.

I

Intention – The power behind Feng Shui. The power of your thoughts and of your attention will enable you to bring about changes you want in life. Thoughts are a form of

energy which can be focused on any object or activity to help you magnify your intention. Any object or activity used for Feng Shui purposes works on your behalf to bring about what you want.

K

Kitchen – Should ideally be in the back of the house away from the front entrance. The health of the food or the act of eating requires privacy otherwise the energy from the front door can overwhelm the food value and its nutrition. Ideally, the kitchen should be primarily white in color with some accent colors of choice. Keeping counter-tops clear and clutter-free can enhance health and creativity.

Knowledge – One of the nine areas of the bagua reflecting learning and education. The Knowledge area is also representative of the inner journey of self-knowledge. The color for Knowledge is blue.

L

Library – A good room to have near the front door, reinforcing the intellectual nature of the inhabitants of the house. Keep only current books, discarding those that have old or outdated ideas.

Lighting – Can be used to create change. Good, deliberate lighting can enhance your ability to "see" more clearly and to be "enlightened" around a goal. All burnt out light bulbs need to be replaced as soon as possible, as well as any lamps or lights that don't work.

M

Mirrors – Should be clear and clean to accurately reflect your intention. Mirrors can enlarge a space, create a new space, make a wall disappear, move a wall, flatten a wall, or deflect negativity. A mirror will do what your intention has directed it to do. Any broken, chipped, cracked mirrors need to be replaced, as do mirror tiles or narrow panels of mirror since you cannot see yourself totally.

Missing Pieces – Denote a challenge or lack in a specific area. When a piece is missing in a home or a room, there may well be a challenge in that area of the bagua. All missing pieces should be addressed to prevent any potential misfortune.

O

Oval Shapes – *See* Round or Oval Shapes.

P

Partnership – One of the nine areas of the bagua, representing personal partners or business partners. The color for Partnership is pink.

Pillars – Round ones preferred. Square pillars create poison arrows (*see* Poison Arrows) causing disturbance and unrest. Round pillars do not have this feature and so are more friendly and workable. Square pillars need to have vines wrapped around them or small white lights. Painted vines would also be effective. Mirrors on all four sides of the square pillar would also negate their effects.

Plants – Are suitable when there's an intention of growth or expansion around an issue. A silk plant may be appropriately substituted where a real one would not do well. Any sickly or dead plants that are being used for Feng Shui must be removed from the area in which they were positioned so they don't adversely affect the issue.

Poison Arrows – Protrusion into a room or space. The corner resulting from this protrusion directs too much hard, fast-moving energy into the space which could affect those sitting or sleeping in its path. A plant placed in front of the corner could soften its impact or a round faceted crystal hanging from the ceiling in front of the corner could negate the effects.

Ponds – Can be advantageous in a garden to enhance the flow of money. Ponds, like birdbaths, need to be filled with fresh, clear water. Having a bubbler or fish in the pond will activate its energy even more.

Pools – *See* Swimming Pools.

R

Red – A favorite Chinese color. The color red can effectively be used for front doors in a residence or business. Even placing pots of red flowers near a front door can be helpful, or a wreath with silk red flowers. Being a quick-action color, it can get energy moving quickly and effectively.

Reputation – *See* Fame & Reputation.

Roads – Act as rivers of energy and can be supportive or challenging. A soft, meandering road or driveway approaching a house is best, for it allows the energy to get there without too much or little movement. When a road or driveway approaches a house head-on, too much energy sweeps over the house or business causing overwhelm. A "protective barrier" needs to be installed to prevent this over-activity. Trees, a hedge or a fountain could

provide the protection a person needs to safely live or work in this situation.

Round or Oval Shapes – Imply harmony, balance, cooperation and conversation. A round or oval table is the best for discussions, meetings and eating meals. Round or oval shapes in the master bedroom enhance the relationship between the couple who sleeps there. Round, faceted crystals add balanced and harmonious energy to a space.

S

Split Entry – Usually splits those entering from something in their lives—their health, their money, a partner, their children, good decisions. Split entries present two staircases immediately upon entrance into the space. One goes up (usually to a living area) and the other goes down (sometimes to a family room or to bedrooms on a lower level). There is always a moment of indecision about where to go when first entering the space. The stair-rail is usually centered in front of the entrance to provide a "splitting" assault when first entering. A round rug or a round faceted crystal hung above the stair rail, even from an existing light fixture, can help ease this tension.

Split Level – Where people operate from different areas in life. A split level has part of the living space on one level and, after ascending or descending a few steps, another part on another level. There are sometimes as many as five various levels from which a person or a family has to operate. This situation is not conducive to unity among those who live there and unity with others outside the family. A round, faceted

crystal in the center of the house will help to balance out the various levels.

Stairs – Carefully placed can be beneficial. When stairs fall in the center of a space, they set up an overall theme of "up and down" with regard to health, as well as money, career, relationships, etc. Ideally a staircase should be built with a gentle turn in it to ease the energy up the stairs. There should be no open risers. They should be well-lit and eventful as a person moves through them, with pictures, color, plants. A staircase situated directly in front of the front doorway invites money and health to exit the space. A round rug or a round faceted crystal between the door and the bottom step can ease this flow.

Statues – Implies heaviness and is therefore appropriate when trying to anchor a situation. A large statue in the Partnership area of the back yard can help to keep a good relationship in place. A statuary image of a deity can likewise anchor a job if placed in the Career area of the space.

Stove – One of the three most important pieces of furniture. (*See* Bed and Desk.) The stove (meaning stovetop, not the oven) has the potential for enhancing money as well as for providing a sense of control in life. Ideally a stovetop should be positioned so that the cook can see the entry doors to the kitchen. When this can't happen, position a mirror so that when facing the stove-top, the cook can see movement behind them and be prepared for any interruptions. Additionally the burners should be kept clean and in working order, rotating the use of all the burners. Using only one or two burners or storing items on some of them, decreases the flow of wealth and should be avoided.

Swimming Pools – Are best if kidney-shaped or rounded. The sharp corners of a pool can create a poison arrow if pointing toward the house, especially a bedroom. A pool is best positioned off the Wealth area of a house.

T

Tables – *See* Round or Oval Shapes.

Toilets – Can create a "drain" in life, particularly when positioned in the center of the space. Keeping the lid down on the toilet and the door closed to the bathroom can lessen the impact of the drainage. A plant (even silk) placed on the back of the toilet tank can also counteract the downward flow of energy. It is important that the plant be growing upward, not a vine trailing downward. Also a mirror hung on the outside of the bathroom door can bounce back any beneficial energy that could be flushed away.

W

Weather Vane – Can be used to activate a "dead end" or to "puncture" the energy of a poison arrow.

Wind chimes – Can be effective when wanting to "call in" a particular situation or thing or whenever the energy seems stagnant. It is important that the wind chime be pleasing to the ear. It is an effective adjustment outside the front door when counteracting the energy from living on a "dead end" street. It can also be used inside or outside a back door that is in the Wealth area of the house or business to prevent money from leaving too quickly. A wind chime can effectively be hung in the Partnership area of a room or a space to "call in" a partner. When angling a bed in a corner of a bedroom, a

wind-chime in the corner will keep it from being dead or stagnant.

Windows – As the "eyes" of the space, they need to be kept clean and repaired. Whenever there's a question around clarity of an issue, washing the windows is an appropriate action to take to get a clear vision. They are also representative of the voice of the children who live in the space. If windows don't operate smoothly or are cracked or boarded up, the children who live there may not be heard. The correct ratio of windows to doors in a room is three to one. If there are more windows than the ratio suggests, the children may be in control. If there are more doors than the ratio suggests, the children again may not be heard.